The Sovereignty of Christ

BY
Ty Ford

Full Circle Publishing
PO BOX 8549
Biloxi, MS 39535
www.juliekeene.com

TXu001970470 / 2015-05-31

Application Title:
Sovereignty with Christ.

Title: Sovereignty with Christ.

Copyright Claimant: John T Ford, 1987- . Address: 6145 Causeyville Rd, Meridian, MS, 39301, United States.

Date of Creation: 2013

Authorship on Application: John T Ford, 1987- ; Citizenship: United States. Authorship: text.

Rights and Permissions: Fourth Day Mininstries, 6145 Causeyville Rd, Meridian, MS, 39301, United States

Names: Ford, John T, 1987

Printed in the United States of America
First Printing, 2017
ISBN-978-0692949511
ISBN-0692949518

ORDERING INFORMATION:

Quantity Sales: Special discounts are available on quantity purchases by corporations, associations, and others via www.tyford.org

Book Cover Design: Full Circle Publishing – Daniel Stombaugh & Julie Keene
Formatting: Daniel Stombaugh
Book Publishing: Full Circle Publishing

Dedication

This Book is Dedicated to my wife, Hillary Ford, and our beautiful children.

All of my family and friends that have stuck by my side and prayed for me when I needed it the most!

Fourth Day Ministries where God has allowed us to be a light in a dark world and lead others to Christ.

Danny and Pam Pierce with Mercy House Ministries for taking me in when nobody else would.

Without the Holy Spirit this book would be full of blank pages so I am grateful for His presence in my life.

Thanks be to you all who have read this book, donated towards it, and became more complete by reading it.

"And I am sure that God, who began the good work within you, will continue His work until it is finally finished on that day when Christ Jesus comes back again."

~Philippians 1:6

GOD CAN TAKE A MESS AND MAKE IT A MIRACLE.

~ TONY EVANS

Introduction

My Story for God's Glory:

I had a pretty good childhood growing up. I was a pretty good kid when I was much younger. I had a love for God. I just never took the time to get to know Him. I was too busy trying to get to know myself and figure out who I was. I didn't realize that the way I figure out who I am is through Him. I got baptized when I was 7. I didn't know what it meant. But, for some reason I felt like it was something I needed to do. I didn't understand church at all when I was growing up. Some kids knew the answer to every biblical question. But not me. It was as if I was lost. I wanted to do right growing up. But, the older I got the harder that was. In middle school I had a couple of minor drinking experiences. I say minor because it wasn't something I did all the time. I had simply taken a couple of shots out of my parents liquor cabinet. But, by the time I was a freshman, I got drunk for my first time. Some friends of mine and I drank a bunch of beer and became pretty intoxicated. I thoroughly enjoyed it. After that, I got high from smoking weed my first time. I enjoyed that as well.

As time went on, I began to look for ways I could get high and drunk without getting caught by my parents. By 10th grade, I took pills my first time. I bought them in math class from a teammate of mine on football team. I bought them with my lunch money. I really loved pills! Throughout high school I would use pills, weed, and alcohol on a regular basis. I played football. By the time I was a junior my dad and neighbor spoke into my life telling me that I had potential to play college ball. It was my dream to play college ball at the University of Southern Mississippi. To make a long story short, I stopped partying so much and began to focus on my dream. My dream became more important to me than partying. I got bigger, faster, and stronger.

I tore my ACL the 3rd game of my senior season. It devastated me. I couldn't bear the thought of having to be done for the year so soon. So, I didn't settle for being out for the season. Instead, I found a doctor in New Orleans that would clear me. This doctor was with the New Orleans Saints. My dad and I had connections through a strength and conditioning coach who helped me train previously. The doctor cleared me and helped me get a knee brace so I could continue playing. The only stipulation was that I would have to rehabilitate the strength in my leg around the knee for 4-5 weeks before getting actually cleared to play. I then finished up the season strong. My knee didn't hold me back much. I started and played every game through the end of the season. We made it to the 3rd round of playoffs where we lost to Pensacola High School. Once the season was over, my desire to party began to creep back up. Then, I got accepted at USM as a preferred walk on. Once that took place my training got more serious than it ever had. I got ACL surgery and hit the ground running! I graduated high school. Then, I went to USM that summer in July.

The workouts were intense. They were challenging. I got to know the rest of the players. I had planned on quitting the party life in order to focus on becoming a stronger athlete. But, once I got there I realized a lot of the players were smoking weed and drinking, so it was hard for me to miss out on that. That's the way I thought at the time. My roommate ended up being a guy I partied with in high school. We ended up doing the same thing in college, except we went even harder in college than we did in high school. We drank. We smoked weed. We took pills. We snorted cocaine. I ended up driving drunk quite often. I wrecked vehicles drunk. I got arrested for possession of alcohol in a dry county once. We went to the bars nearly every night. At that point, I was hanging on by a thread with school and football. My dream was no longer more important than partying. It's as if the strongholds in my life got to a point where they weighed so heavy on me that I didn't have the strength to fight them off. I became known as a guy who liked to party. In fact, a friend of mine started a Facebook group called "You haven't partied until you've partied with

8

Ty Ford." Then in the group under the description, it went on to say, "He puts the T Y in party." My identity was in football. Then it was in partying.

But soon after, I got kicked off the football team for failing 5 drug tests. I was selling drugs at that point. I felt so lost after losing my spot on the team. Every bit of accountability I had, I lost. It was devastating. Yet, I went on with my life as if I hadn't cared. Then, selling drugs and partying was all I did. I failed out of school. I went back home to Destin, FL. I sold drugs there and partied. I worked little jobs here and there. But, really the only reason I worked the jobs I did was to finance my partying and financially back my drug selling. My life drastically went downhill. I was bound up and didn't know how to get out. This lasted for a couple of years. I sold drugs. I got robbed one time. So, I moved to Memphis to lay low for a while.

One weekend I came back to Destin and I had a bad sea doo accident where I suffered a severe brain injury. Life really got hard then. But in the midst of that accident I heard from God. God told me it wasn't my time yet. He said I had something to share with the world. That really confused me at the time because I didn't understand what that meant. But, years later I realized it was Him I was to share with the world. Also, my testimony. The trauma to my head caused me to be wild and "out there." It hurt and I used drugs to cope with the pain. I ended up going to several psych wards over a course of a few years. The doctors put me on all kinds of crazy medicines. Then, I got arrested for possession of cocaine. I would use cocaine a lot to help cope with my chemical imbalance that was caused by the head trauma. The brain is a very difficult thing to understand. I believe God had to let my bump my head real hard to wake me up. It is still my thorn to this very day. My journey after the wreck went from bad to worse. I sold drugs on a big scale. I lived in California for a few years and one week I made $25,000. I also began shooting heroin and cocaine as an IV user.

This went on for years. My sister Erin kept planting seeds with me about Jesus Christ. She said whenever I was ready to give my life to Christ He would help me see myself the way He sees me. So, one night I laid in my bed strung out on drugs thinking about what my future looked like. At that time it wasn't too promising. I had just robbed several drug dealers and I was living in Destin at the time. Destin wasn't too big of a place. I felt like I was going to have to keep looking over my shoulder. So, there I was laying in my bed as I reached my hand up and said, "Jesus, take the reins of my life even if I have to go to jail and detox from heroin and cocaine. If that's what it takes, so be it! I want to live a life that serves you and experience what you have for me. Take me away from here!" God is all about specifics. A week and a half later I went to jail.

From jail, I went to Mercy House Ministries in Hurley, MS in October 2012. Danny Pierce and his wife extended the grace to me to allow me to come into their program. I'm forever grateful. I'm forever indebted to them for what that place did in my life. It is a 12-15 month long program. It's associated with Teen Challenge international. I went there for a year and graduated. I fell in love with God and was able to love myself in a healthy way like never before.

I memorized scripture. I learned biblical principles. I was challenged. It was great! God even gave me a vision for my ministry, Fourth Day Ministries. After graduating, I went on to work as a staff member at Mercy House. I learned the ministry as I was promoted to Marketing Director, then Assistant Program Director. God used that year of being a staff member to help equip me for my ministry. At Fourth Day Ministries, we have given away over 1,000 study Bibles so far. We have a house we have used to help men transition from faith based rehabs back into society. We help the men get jobs, we disciple them, we help them save their money, and we help lead them into answering God's call on their lives. We evangelize by going to different places and sharing our testimonies while also speaking God's truth. We have a piece of property now in Meridian, MS that used to be a Girl Scout Camp, but is now ours to be used for giving

God glory. We are setting it up for camps and retreats. We had our first camp in July 2017, and it was a great success. A high school football team came in and I was privileged enough to speak to them and share what God has done in my life. God has turned all things around for His good. He turned my mess into ministries. I also now have a wife and 3 beautiful children. God has truly blessed us. On September 24, 2017 I will have been clean and sober for 5 years. I give Him all the glory! May The Lord speak to you as you read this book. May what He speaks to you change your life. He changed mine, and I haven't been disappointed ever since!

"IF IT WEREN'T FOR SOMEONE ELSE'S FAITH AND OBEDIENCE, I WOULD HAVE NEVER UNDERSTOOD WHO JESUS IS AND WOULD HAVE NEVER GOTTEN SAVED. I CERTAINLY WOULDN'T BE WRITING THIS BOOK FOR ALL OF YOU RIGHT NOW."

~ TY FORD

CHAPTER ONE:
Living as Citizens of Heaven

We all belong to a particular community, city, town, state, country, or even an organization. We either belong there because that's where we usually stay, or that's what we represent. If you are from Mexico, you probably speak Spanish just like if you are from America, you probably speak English. Hispanics eat a little different from Americans, just like Americans typically eat different from Hispanics. Both parties may enjoy eating some of the same types of food. However, the point is that each different citizen walks a little different, talks a little different, and eats a little bit differently because of the way they are made and the way they were brought up.

We are all citizens of Heaven once we have accepted Christ as our Lord and Savior. That's why it's important to resemble "Whose" we are.

If you have not accepted Christ as your Lord and Savior yet, you will certainly have the opportunity to do it now, and I encourage you to not hesitate. If you're not ready yet, that is understandable; but I encourage you not to wait too long. God's plan will always trump our own. Be bold!

"For if you confess with your mouth that Jesus is Lord and believe in your heart that God raised Him from the dead, you will be saved. For it is by believing in your heart that you are made right with God, and it is by confessing with your mouth that you are saved."

~ Romans 10: 9-10

Once you declare that Jesus is your Lord, He will then be your Savior. Accept Him into your life in such a way that you receive Him as Lord and let Him take the reins of your life in such a way that you follow His guidance.

"For everyone who calls on the Name of The Lord will be saved."

~ **Romans 10:13**

The blood of Jesus Christ saves us from the wrath of our Heavenly Father.

"For we all have sinned and fall short of the glory of God, being justified as a gift by His grace, through the redemption which is in Christ Jesus"

~ **Romans 3:23-24**

In other words, we all have sinned but thank God for His only Son, Jesus Christ. We have all been born into "iniquity," but freedom comes through the blood of Jesus Christ. It is crucial we receive His blood for forgiveness of our sins. It's a decision *only you can make for yourself.* We will all one day give a personal account in the face of Christ on that day of judgement.

Those who receive, believe, and continuously **obey** Jesus Christ as their Lord *will walk through the pearly gates and onto the streets of gold.* All whose names are written in the Book of Life will be given this privilege.

The greatest part of Heaven will not be pearly gates or streets of gold, but the Presence of The Lord.

*It will be a dreadful day of Judgement for those who **do not** continuously obey Christ as Lord of their lives, for they will be sent to eternal condemnation.*

John 15 tells us the importance of "lasting fruit." It doesn't stop at the cross. *It starts there.* We must take up our cross and follow Jesus.

Luke 14:25-33 gives us insight for the cost of discipleship and also stresses the importance of finishing what we started:

"Now huge crowds were going along with [Jesus], and He turned and said to them, If anyone comes to Me and does not hate his [own] father and mother [in the sense of indifference to or relative disregard for them in comparison with his attitude toward God] and [likewise] his wife and children and brothers and sisters--[yes] and even his own life also--he cannot be My disciple. Whoever does not persevere and carry his own cross and come after (follow) Me cannot be My disciple. For which of you, wishing to build a farm building, does not first sit down and calculate the cost [to see] whether he has sufficient means to finish it? Otherwise, when he has laid the foundation and is unable to complete [the building], all who see it will begin to mock and jeer at him, Saying, This man began to build and was not able (worth enough) to finish. Or what king, going out to engage in conflict with another king, will not first sit down and consider and take counsel whether he is able with ten thousand [men] to meet him who comes against him with twenty thousand? And if he cannot [do so], when the other king is still a great way off, he sends an envoy and asks the terms of peace. So then, any of you who does not forsake (renounce, surrender claim to, give up, say good-bye to) all that he has cannot be My disciple."

~ Luke 14:25 - 14:33 (AMP)

Salvation comes through receiving Jesus as Lord. Therefore, it is important to ***keep Him as Lord!***

"My sheep hear My voice, and I know them, and they follow Me, and I give eternal life to them, and none of them shall ever perish, and no one shall snatch them out of My hand."

~ John 10:27-28

As long as we have the desire to follow Jesus, we will search out His truth and ways through His Word. His Word will point us in the right direction.

"Your Word is a lamp for my feet and light for my path." In other words, His truth reveals to us where we are and guides us into the direction we must go. Obeying His Word draws us closer to Him because obedience honors the *relationship* we have with Him. As we draw closer to Him, He draws closer to us. This causes the enemy of our soul to flee.

~ Psalm 119:105

"So humble yourselves before God. Resist the devil, and he will flee from you. Come close to God, and God will come close to you. Wash your hands, you sinners; purify your hearts, for your loyalty is divided between God and the world."

~ James 4:7-8

As we humble ourselves before God, we **submit** to Him. This means we are in **submission** to His will, His ways, and in agreement with His Word. When we do **submit to God** in such a way, we are walking with the **power and authority** of the *Holy Spirit*! We have dominion and power over the enemy when we are walking in **obedience to God**. We are capable of saying, **"*Get behind me Satan!*"** The enemy of our soul must obey us when we speak by the **authority of the Holy Spirit!** Dolphins are known for often times protecting humans from shark attacks. Some say it's the **sound** that dolphins make.

As God's children, proclaiming the Word of God is a mighty weapon we have access to for protecting ourselves against the evil one. Ephesians 6:17 says, "*Put on salvation as your helmet, and take the **sword of the Spirit,** which is the **Word of God**.*" This sword of the Spirit is our only ***weapon of offense***. This is the **Word of God** and His Word is **light**. *Light overpowers darkness every time*. The helmet of salvation reminds us "Whose we are!" It's *important we "remain in His love" by obeying His commands.*

Walking in obedience to God is not a matter of perfection, but rather a mindset and/or mentality. Obedience is not based on *performance*. Obedience is a condition which is sown into a man's heart. Obedience to God is based on **faithfulness**.

When we confess Jesus as Lord, we make a **vow** to Him and are **saved**. *When two get married they become one.* At a wedding, the man and the woman both say their **vows**. Marriage vows consists of a mutual agreement between the two parties, centered on love and faithfulness. However, if the man is faithful and the woman is not, adultery happens. Marriage is designed by God to be a blood covenant with Him and with one another. A blood covenant is a close relationship between two parties where blood is shed, two become one, and all possessions are shared upon demand. For example, a man marries a woman, and a virgin bride would shed blood at the time of intimacy. Their blood covenant portrays their love for one another in a faithful manner where all they own or possess is to be shared upon demand. And, this is held sacred by God.

Another example: Jesus Christ died a criminals death as an innocent man, Who also was God in the flesh. This is a blood covenant that covers the iniquities of man, supplying eternal life for man with God. **Jesus Christ as Lord is a blood covenant because Christ has died and shed blood as a sinner so that we sinners may be made right with God through His blood.** God remains faithful even when we become unfaithful. *It is the goodness of God that brings man into repentance.* There is no such thing as being 100% obedient 24/7. We all fall short at times. But, how faithful are we over the course of this journey and in the long haul of this race? Obedience is empowered by **faith** and made possible through God's grace. Salvation is a free gift from God that is received by **faith**. When we wake up in the morning and say, "Thank You Jesus for waking me up this morning and designing my day to be filled with opportunities for me to speak and act in such a way that honors You and gives You glory!" We talk to God by **faith**. We pray to God **faithfully**. We plant seeds in others by sharing our testimonies because of the *faith He has placed inside of us*. A *relationship* built with somebody is built by spending time with one another. God wants us to spend time with Him. As we spend time with Him, He gives us spiritual strength and confidence to boldly love others the way He loves us. Our *relationship* involves *commitment*. *In order for one to be committed to a relationship, they must be diligent. Diligence in a relationship involves faithfulness.* David was a man after God's own heart. David had many quirks, falls, and failures. But, there was a condition sown into his heart that inspired him to keep on chasing after God! David had a mentality that would not allow him to relent and give up on the relationship with God he had started. *David chased after God and lived a life that revealed the fruits of repentance.* He fell short many times just as we all do.

However, he continued to build on the relationship with God he first had as a young boy. He was driven by a heart for obedience that God had put there. God had sown into David's heart a condition that desired nothing more than to be obedient to his Lord, Savior, and King.

Love God with all your heart, mind, soul, and strength. Love others the way Christ loves you. The more we **get to know** God through praying and reading His Word, the more we love Him. The more time we spend with God, the more we recognize how boundless His love for us is. The more our spiritual eyes and spiritual ears tune into Christ, the more love we receive. As a result, we love others greater because our perception of love has become enhanced and further known. Then, we are more capable of loving others as we are commanded by God to do. There is an **overflow** effect to an **intimate** relationship with Christ. Intimacy with God involves praying, meditating, and studying His Word while recognizing His presence. He is everywhere all of the time. He lives in us all. Once we receive Him as Lord of our lives, we are then empowered by His Holy Spirit Who comforts us, guides us, convicts us, and counsels us. It is great to take a few deep breaths and tune into the **dimension** of His holy presence.

I encourage this before studying His Word so that you may receive an impartation to your heart from His truth. Without the awareness of God's presence, studying His Word is just head knowledge from *text*. But, with the awareness of His presence when studying His Word, there is an *impartation* that takes place!

Once you have accepted your new life, granted through God's forgiveness and His plan of redemption, you become a "Citizen of Heaven."

The New Jerusalem mentioned in the book of Revelation is actually Heaven itself.

"And the twelve gates were twelve pearls, each of the gates made of a single pearl, and the street of the city was pure gold, like transparent glass."

~ Revelation 21:21

Pure gold down here on earth is expensive, but in the New Jerusalem (a.k.a. Heaven), that is what us children of God will be stomping all over with our feet! Heaven is unimaginable! Once we "Citizens of Heaven" reach our destination, we will literally be blown away beyond what our imagination can even fathom. Why not give this a shot? I did! And, Christ has not let me down yet. I am convinced He never will! He has carried me through much adversity and has also taught me a lot. I'm still not fully finished, but He has molded me into an entirely new creation far from the creature I used to be!

"And I am sure that God, who began the good work within us will continue His work until it is finally finished on that day when Christ Jesus comes back again."

~ Philippians 1:6

Sovereignty of Christ

The Kingdom of God lives in all the hearts of the redeemed. In order for His Kingdom to come and His will to be done on earth as it is in Heaven, the Bride of Christ must be faithful in divine opportunities. The saved are called to represent Christ and no longer resemble the ways of the world.

"And do not be conformed to this world, but be transformed by the renewing of your mind, that you may prove what is that good and acceptable and perfect will of God."

~ Romans 12:2 (NKJV)

We are called to a life of transformation, not conformation. We are to be reformed and not conformed. We are to be consecrated and set apart from the world, NOT of the world. We are chosen to be a light in the midst of a dark world with the purpose of reconciling the "broken" back to God through Jesus Christ!

So, what is it that we are required to do as Christians? There's not as much to it as most would say. However, Jesus says for us to love Him above all other gods and love our neighbors as ourselves. And, He also says, "Love each other as I have loved you. By doing this, you will prove to the world that you are My disciples" (John 13: 34, 35). Our lives ought to uphold Christ-like character and we have been chosen to represent Him in the way we live. Love, joy, peace, faithfulness, patience, gentleness, kindness, goodness, and self-control all represent His character as these 9 characteristic traits are the "Fruit of the Holy Spirit" (Galatians 5:22, 23). People are always observing others. When I see a Hispanic person, I notice they are Hispanic.

When Hispanic people see me, they notice I am an American. It's very obvious! We are called to live lives that **represent Christ** in an *obvious* manner as well!

"So we are Christ's ambassadors; God is making His appeal through us. We speak for Christ when we plead, 'Be reconciled to God!'"

~ 2 Corinthians 5:20

We are ALL called to be "ministers of reconciliation". Salvation through His sacrifice on the cross ought to inspire us to be of *greater* service to others! There is no greater love than to lay our lives down for our friends (John 15:13). God is faithful!

We are all unique individuals with interesting personalities. Some personalities are more interesting than others. Nonetheless, God will equip us to serve Him and give us each individually an anointing by the measure of His grace. The purpose of His anointing is to break all yokes of bondage and strengthen us for the call. God has called us to be interactive and relational with Himself as well as with others. As we are interactive and relational with others, establishing common ground is a great icebreaker! *Discover the interests of those you interact with.* Ask The Lord for a way to speak into the lives of others so they will be able to easily grasp and understand the love of Christ.

Also, activities and recreation are a great way to establish relationships. Fishing, hiking, sports, and hunting are great ways to build relationships and have clean fun!

Am I a Christian today? Absolutely, but that doesn't mean I forgot what it was like to be a sinner. As I witness to unbelievers, I witness to them in such a way where I put myself in their shoes by first thinking back to what it was like to be an unbeliever, denying the fact God had a purpose for my life. In parallel terms, an old drug dealer that changed to become a narcotics agent is very much similar to a sinner that got saved to lead other sinners to salvation through Jesus Christ. That narcotics agent will always remember what dealing drugs was like and how he tried to get away with it. So, he would reflect back on what he used to do in order to give him insight for the assignments he's been called to do. It hasn't been so long ago for me that I forgot how I used to think while I was living in sin and rebellion. I remember how I thought. I remember what I thought of people who were sold out to Jesus. Now I am the one who is ***sold out to Jesus,*** set out on a mission to exemplify the truth and reality of the

Resurrection of Christ to other people who are like the old me. Would you be interested in pursuing your calling?

You may be like the old me, just dancing around the idea of salvation in reading this book or you may be just how I am now; on fire for God burning with purpose! Either way, you are all called! Whether you are **chosen** will depend on if you pick up the telephone or not and tell the King of Kings and Lord of Lord's you will show up for the assignments He's calling you to do. If you are simply dancing around the idea on *salvation*, call on Jesus out loud and tell Him you want Him to take the reins of your life. See what happens! I guarantee that when you *genuinely* do, you will find new life and an *abundance* of it! It's a beautiful blessing! Study the Word and educate yourself enough to have a better understanding of your new life and prepare yourself for the mighty calling God has on your life.

"Only let your conversation be as it becomes the Gospel of Christ: that whether I come and see you, or else be absent, I may hear of your affairs, that you stand fast in one spirit, with one mind striving together for the Faith of the Gospel."

~ Philippians 1:27

"Conversation" can also mean "lifestyle," which is telling us to be **"doers of God's Word."** *The ultimate memoir of our "new life" or "salvation" is exclusively The Cross and what Christ did there.* When the enemy, Satan, attacks us over and over again; all we have to do is think of what the *cross* represents. That is forgiveness, freedom, and healing! Thank God for His plan of redemption; sending His Spirit incarnated as the flesh of a man, *JESUS*, and dying a horrific death just so we can live eternally free from sin and destruction. *The cost for God was much, but it costs us little.*

All we have to do is accept God's offering of forgiveness and salvation so that we are then capable of walking out the **fruits of repentance**, and *fruitful obedience*. As we do, our objectives are very similar. We all make up different stones of the Temple, Christ being the Cornerstone. If you haven't received Christ as your Savior yet, an interesting tip is Psalms 118:22.

"The stone which the builders rejected has become the chief cornerstone."

~ Psalms 118:22

The Pharisees were typically hypocrites that faked a holy life and most all of them rejected Jesus, the *Cornerstone*. The most religious people back then were the ones that were sticklers to the law yet rejected their own Savior! Go figure... But, learn from those people who refused the Head Stone, being Jesus. We all need Jesus because He has paid a debt none of us could pay. He paid all of our debts and all we have to do is *individually* receive. When we recognize what He has already **done** for us, we ought to strongly desire to serve Him. I encourage you all to live a life to the fullest and strive to become closer to God each and every day. If you are naturally led to refuse Christ, then recognize that as your own natural inclination. Because of Adam, we are naturally inclined to live sinfully, be ashamed, then go into hiding. *However, due to our iniquities we are in desperate need of a Lord and Savior!* Sin is in our heritage, but that doesn't give us a reasonable excuse to blatantly allow it to rule our lives and control the way we live.

Sin is destructive and ends with death but Jesus is holy and a life with Him never ends.

"Since you have been raised to new life with Christ, set your sights on the realities of Heaven, where Christ sits in the place of honor at God's right hand."

~ Colossians 3:1

23

Sovereignty of Christ

We have been risen with Christ, so "Yes..." Why not seek things that are above? Things that come from above are like "peace, joy, patience, faith, love, gentleness, goodness, kindness, and self-control" (Galatians 5:22,23). What man can pass down anything like that to us? No man except Jesus, whom is God! In John 14:6, Jesus tells us, "I am the way, the truth, and the life. No one comes to the Father, except through Me."

Speaking of a "New Life,"

"Are you ignorant of the fact that all of us who have been baptized into Christ Jesus were baptized into His death? We were buried therefore with Him by the baptism into death, so that just as Christ was raised from the dead by the glorious [power] of the Father, so we too might [habitually] live and behave in newness of life. For if we have become one with Him by sharing a death like His, we shall also be [one with Him in sharing] His resurrection [by a new life lived for God."

~ Romans 6:3-5

In other words, our sinful lives have died with Christ when He died. Just as He overcame death, we too may live new lives.

"set our affection on things above, not on things of this earth."

~ Colossians 3:2

Therefore, it is evident that our main source of help comes from God and there is limited amount of help on earth. A lot of the time, God may work through someone on earth to help us out, but without God's help, those people would not have ever been *led* to do so.

"For you are dead, and your life is hid with Christ in God."

~ Colossians 3:3

24

We are dead to our old lives because Jesus died on the Cross as if we died with Him. In other words, He took our old lives with Him to the Cross, but as He rose up from the dead, death has been overcome in Jesus' name! Jesus takes us as we are, but then sets us free and sends on a mission with a new name.

Paul was Saul before Christ. Our whole identity changes once we receive Christ! We must then discover who we really are by spending time with Him. Understand that *citizenship* may have its different waves of circumstances, but your identity remains the same. If you are an American citizen but got arrested and went to jail, your circumstances would change but your citizenship would remain the same. You will go through trials and may experience some seasons of battling strongholds. But stand firm on your identity in Christ as a *heavenly citizen*, and allow Him to set you free! Whenever you have prayed all you can pray, stand and wait for God to fight your battles for you so that victory will be yours in Jesus Name!

Remember Christ's command concerning our love for each other:

"I have a new commandment for you. Love one another as I have loved you. By doing this, you will prove to the world you are My disciples"

~John 13:34,35

Now pay the love forward that you already have received and trust in Jesus Christ as your Lord to give you more! He gives the Holy Spirit to us so that we are **empowered** to do His will according to His ways and in His strength. As we have been promised eternal life through a tenacious act of faithful obedience by Jesus Christ, we must do something with the lives we have left down here on earth. If your brother or sister took a bullet for you, would you not honor his/her life for the rest of yours?

Exactly!

Jesus is our older brother and we are all children of the same Father. Now let's live honorable lives to pay our respect to such an honorable man whom is our God, Jesus Christ Himself. God wants to have an intimate relationship with everyone. Sadly enough, not everyone will accept Him into their lives, but we can at least make sure that several do. Right!? If it weren't for someone else's faith and obedience, I would have never understood who Jesus is and would have never gotten saved. I certainly wouldn't be writing this book for all of you right now.

But you see, someone did take the time and patience to deal with me. Danny Pierce is a mighty Man of God that helped me walk into the *call* upon my life. He encouraged me! He inspired me! He loved me! He taught me the importance of following the Holy Spirit. What a blessing it is to be a child of God. There is so much joy pumping through my veins as I write this book to help all of you! I am an **heir of Christ** grateful to be used, and I hope to be used by Him more and more every day. What I want most, is for every reader to be encouraged. Seek understanding to the call God has on your life and become fulfilled with Grace that empowers you to go and do great things for God's Kingdom! The Word of God is what feeds us faith.

"Faith comes by hearing, and hearing by the Word of God"

~Romans 10:17

This book is only a snack compared to the real thing. The real thing is the Word of God. I encourage you all to read His Word!

When you do, take a couple deep breaths and recognize the **presence of God**. His presence is everywhere all of the time. He's in us living on the inside and He's so much greater than anything of the world that's on the outside. Read His Word and don't get in a hurry. Read His Word and take notes with a pencil or pen. Don't get overwhelmed in fear of making a mistake in the things you may jot down. But write down whatever comes to mind as you read and think. Allow your heart to receive the impartation of truth in His word. As you do, write your impressions down.

CHAPTER 2:
Shine Bright For Christ!

What's more attractive? Light or night? If you stay in a dark room long enough, you will become depressed. Who wants that? Bright sunny days illuminate the beauty of all creation. Darkness hides it. However, there is a need for both in our world.

"Darkness as black as night covers all the nations of the earth, but the glory of the Lord rises and appears over you."

~ Isaiah 60:2

As citizens of Heaven, we shine brightest to those who are dying in darkness. Christ uses us to reach out to them. Too much light can be bad and an excessive amount of darkness is never good. But, when you can be an instrument God uses to illustrate the light of His Kingdom, why settle for less?

There is enough darkness in today's world, spiritually speaking. Therefore, wouldn't it be better to strive towards something better like "shining bright for Christ?"

There is a very high demand for this in God's Kingdom. Unfortunately, there aren't as many people willing to make the sacrifices necessary in order to carry out such a demand. I want you to realize that you don't necessarily have to make "sacrifices," just a "sacrifice." The main sacrifice is obedience with a thankful attitude. There's a lot we can thank God for, but to sum it up, His Grace is the **main thing** to be thankful for. Let's keep the **main thing** the **"main thing."** Let us understand God's grace as we navigate towards a 2 Corinthians 8:9 mindset.

27

"For we know the Grace of our Lord Jesus Christ, that, though He was rich, yet for your sakes He became poor, that you through His poverty might be rich."

~2 Corinthians 8:9

In other words, Christ gave Himself up to this world, where He came from an unimaginable place full of all riches (known as Heaven) that stomp on our little bit of riches we have here. He became poor and endured the most horrible death ever just so we could be made right with God and inherit His will. He died as us so that we could be set free through Him. He paid the price, which conquered death, hell, and the grave. Through Him we are free from all three! All we have to do is *accept Him* as our own Lord and Savior. It's historically proven that Jesus Christ was crucified, died, was buried, and somehow appeared to approximately 500 people in a wonderfully majestic, glorious body that no one even knew how to explain! The same power that raised Christ from the dead back then also lives in all who believe today. People literally claimed to have seen Him with their own eyes and all their stories matched up. The disciple Thomas didn't even believe it was Jesus until he stuck his fingers in Jesus' holes on His wrists! Could you imagine? A dead guy showing up on your front porch and you think you're just having a flashback or something, but then he talks to you... Plus you are able to touch the holes in His wrists and feel the reality of *life*. That's crazy!

There are respectable scientists these days that have gone from atheists to Christians based on their own discovery through intensive research. They say, "It takes more faith to believe in natural selection than a higher deity." That's interesting. However, don't be alarmed by the usual stubborn atheist. There's also a lot of people who believe in other religions. God bless them, but those other religions mostly began with rebellion against the Living God.

Living for God gives you this conviction to love all people, no matter what race they are, their sexual orientation, or religion they are involved in. Grace *propels* us to live a godly life with moral excellence and later self-control. Don't you see, Jesus went from being rich to humbling Himself, by paying the high cost for us to have an opportunity to live eternally with Him. Don't get it twisted; we all have eternal life regardless! If you just want to die and rest in peace, too bad because that's not an option! It's either rejecting Christ and going to Hell **or** accepting Him and going to Heaven. Watch at how Jesus puts this in Matthew 20:28.

"Just as the Son of Man did not come to be served, but to serve and give His life, a ransom for many."

~ Matthew 20:28

Jesus was not a mooch. He is Jehovah Jireh, *The Lord Who Provides!*

If you are a mother who likes to shop and you find a hot sale, do you call any friends and tell them about it so they can get in on it too? I sure hope you do! When I was an alcoholic and addict, if I found a good deal or a great "Happy Hour," I always called at least 20 people and told them where they needed to be! But hey, that's just me. Now I have found Heaven on earth which leads to the *Real* Heaven I'm destined to go to, so that's why I am reaching out to all of you. I am going, but I want every single one of you to go with me! I not only want you to come with me, but I also want you to call all of your friends, so they can call all their friends, and etc., because that's where the *Real Party* is! Ain't no party like a Holy Ghost party because a Holy Ghost party don't stop!

Sometimes I get selfish and wish I'd get to go to Heaven sooner, but I must put myself in check with the realization that I have much more to do before I can go. I just won't die until my mission here is *finished* like what Jesus said on The Cross. It must be *finished*!

I have to be very careful how I carry myself and watch what I say and be cautious of everything I do because guess what? Folks are

29

watching! But, that is nothing new. People have been watching me my whole life, whether it be my friends, or their parents, or my family or sometimes even the cops too. Either way, people watch other people. I really like to people watch.

"In everything you do, stay away from complaining and arguing so that no one can speak a word of blame against you. You are to live clean, innocent lives as children of God in a dark world full of people who are crooked and stubborn" (New Living Bible).

~ Philippians 2:14,15

If I were to cuss like a sailor, someone would hear about it and it would get to my church, somehow! I don't want even a gang member to hear me cuss because I am just as much interested in leading him to Christ as anyone else. Something as simple as foul language can discredit our witness to someone. We must be wise, harmless, and careful. We don't want to hinder anyone from getting to know Christ. In Christ, we are His ambassadors on this earth!

The ministry I used to work for, *Mercy House Ministries*, has many men that come onto the property from all types of different backgrounds. Gang-like street affiliation is very common. They are no different than me or anybody else who has been through the type of ringer I'm talking here. We have all made mistakes! But guess what!? Jesus paid for all our transgressions, our mistakes, our sins, our whatever you choose to call it! He paid for mine. He pays for killers! He chose me. He chooses them. He's already chosen you. But, just because He has chosen you does not mean He can do it all for you. You have to live up to what being *chosen* is all about. It's about accepting the sacrifice of Jesus Christ, in all His sovereignty, and making the sacrifice of "obedience" with gratitude! What are you going to do? You have one life. Time is ticking!

There's temptations that want to strike a match with me every day. It is a battle zone everywhere I go... Sex, cigarettes, drinking, drugs, dealing, anger, pride, gambling, manipulations, fighting, and everything else all tempt me. But, just because all those send me invitations every day does not mean that my one good invitation that really matters doesn't count any more. That invitation is "Heaven." There's no party on earth worth missing the *Real Party* in Heaven for. I thought I had all my fun in the world until I gave my life to Christ, and *fun* then had just began! Winning *Souls to Christ* is what I call fun! I don't keep count because that's not my part. I choose to bring souls to Jesus and let Him do the counting. My focus is simply that every life counts! I do try to gather an idea of the count on who's not there yet and reach out to people of that party more because people that have Jesus only need reiteration, but people who don't have Jesus need to get introduced to Him. Let me introduce you to Him as you read this book.

When we recognize the character of Jesus Christ; we see tenacity, strength, love, boldness, and humility. *Sovereignty* means supreme power or authority.

"As he came to the towns of Bethphage and Bethany on the Mount of Olives, he sent two disciples ahead. 'Go into that village over there,' he told them. 'As you enter it, you will see a young donkey tied there that no one has ever ridden. Untie it and bring it here. If anyone asks, 'Why are you untying that colt?' just say, 'The Lord needs it.' So they went and found the colt, just as Jesus had said. And sure enough, as they were untying it, the owners asked them, 'Why are you untying that colt?' And the disciples simply replied, 'The Lord needs it.'"

~Luke 19:29 - 34 (NLT).

There is "*Sovereignty*" in Christ! His instructions and promises will never fail us! He is the Name above all names! He is the author of salvation! He is the perfecter of faith! He is The Lord Who heals. He is The Lord Who sanctifies! He sanctifies us by His truth! He makes us holy by His Spirit!

31

His presence empowers us to overcome greed and become content with little, much, or nothing. Jesus Christ is the Almighty, Powerful, and Living God! There is always someone who just has to pull out in front of us on the interstate going 45 mph when we have the cruise control set at 80. But, His goodness brings us to repentance. Where we used to blatantly sin, His goodness inspires us to no longer do so.

There's times of stress ahead. There's temptations of greed at every crossroad after a blessing. However, life is full of choices. When we recognize the goodness of God, we are intrigued and guided by His nature. We live in a vicious world full of confused people who think it is okay and normal to be guided by evil. There are people you make extra efforts to please who may stab you in the back, figuratively speaking.

"If anyone mistreats you because you are a Christian, don't curse them. Pray that God will bless them."

~ Romans 12:14

This is the hardest thing to do. We live in a dark world, yet we are called to shine as bright lights when we totally commit to living for Christ. When I first became active in my faith, I was trying so hard to change and make certain adjustments in my life that weren't easy. So, since I was trying so hard and working hard at it, my expectations for other people's behavior was so high. Funny how that works, but it is true. I held people to a standard almost higher than the same one I was holding myself to. It got hard a lot of times to keep my temper. When I went through Mercy House, I "got into it" with almost every staff member at least a couple times! I was so frustrated by what they did that I messed up and bucked their authority, rather than submitting to it as I am required to by the teaching of God's Word. Now that I am in their same position, I realize just how ridiculous I must have looked. Nonetheless, this walk with Christ involves humility and growth. Sometimes we must be humiliated before we actually grow.

We will talk more about "submitting to authority" in another chapter as that's part of "surrendering to God." I just want you to realize how crucial it is for us as Christians to not "react" so fast to what others say or do to us because our reaction or response can either turn them away from the truth or turn them onto the truth. Which would we rather it be? Obviously, the main objective is to turn others on to the truth and live a life that is appealing to them so that when they find out we are Christians, they will become interested in the same lifestyle we live. The truth set me free. Has it set you free? Have you discovered the truth yet?

Well if you haven't, then I definitely recommend for you to get a New Living Translation Study Bible. If you need help finding one, I will be happy to help out. God recently birthed a ministry through me called *Fourth Day Ministries*. A big portion of what this ministry is all about is giving Study Bibles for those in need. Life Application Study Bibles provide extra commentary and footnotes to help readers further understand the Gospel in such a way that empowers them to apply it to their lives.

The New Living Translation is a version that is in modern English terms so we may understand the context much better as it also sticks to the root meaning of original Hebrew and Greek text. If you take the "text" out of *context,* you are left with "con." Therefore, it is better to develop a clear understanding of the text so that you are not "conned."

There's much more to being a Christian than just *accepting* Him as our Lord and Savior. It is evidently, as we mentioned, also about "shining bright for Him." His Grace goes far beyond measure and the things I am doing today are made possible through His Grace. His Grace propels us in such a way that we live a totally different life. A life that we are totally content with! You don't have to change to accept Christ. Once you accept Christ, He will empower you by His grace to change!

33

Sovereignty of Christ

The Study Bible giving part of Fourth Day Ministries has impacted the lives of many! There's no greater gift than a good study Bible that a person can clearly understand. If you are interested in sowing into this ministry you may visit :

"www.fourthdayministries.org"

and click the tab "donate." Also, if you are interested in receiving a Study Bible because you are in need, please email **"fourthdayministries@gmail.com"** and we will do our best in helping meet the need.

CHAPTER 3:
A Life Lived with Humility

I have learned over the years that it is truly hard to let go completely of all lethal pride. What is lethal pride? What is healthy pride? Well, healthy pride is when you are doing something great and you take pride in it!

Take your job for example. If you clean windows for a living, it's honorable to do a great job and take pride in the work that you do. I work at a ministry that caters to men's lives, and I take pride in it because in order for me to take pride in what I do, I must do a great job! So, it is healthy for me to be prideful in such a way because it drives me to increase my productivity.

Satan got himself kicked out of God's Kingdom because his pride was lethal. He wanted to take over and he took over alright! But, he did not take over the Kingdom of God. He only took over all evil. That's not a very honorable job to have!

"How are you fallen from Heaven, O Lucifer, son of the morning! how are you cut down to the ground, which did weaken the nations! For you have said in your heart, I will ascend into Heaven, I will exalt my throne above the stars of God: I will sit also upon the mount of the congregation, in the sides of the north: I will ascend above the heights of the clouds; I will be like the Most High. Yet you shall be brought down to Hell, to the sides of the pit.

~ Isaiah 14: 12-15

Lucifer, as most of you already know, is Satan. Lucifer was his name as an angel of the Kingdom before his rebellion. About one-third of the angels followed him. Therefore, all the misery and heartaches, pain and suffering, death and deception are a result of his revolution against The Almighty, Living God. He wanted to be above all the stars of God, meaning he wanted to be number 1 without cooperation! It was all about him, and his plans were more important to him than God's plan. He exalted himself by idolizing himself instead of devoted worship to God. After his fall, he deceived other angels to follow him in his rebellious revolution.

With all this being said, we can break it down like this. A football team has an offensive side and also a defensive side. The defense has someone call the plays just like the offense does. The quarterback calls the huddle on the offensive side, and the middle linebacker usually calls the huddle for the defense. The quarterback touches the ball every play, and the middle linebacker typically gets the most tackles. However, for some teams they don't because either they don't have a great player playing that position or their defense is ran a little different. Some run a 4-3 defense and some run a 4-4. Others run 4-2-5 and some run a 5-2. It just depends. Anyway, most quarterbacks and middle linebackers have a pretty good sized ego. How do I know?

Well, I played Middle Linebacker for nearly 11 years and I still have that mentality. Through my walk with Christ, I have learned to be more humble, but I am still guilty of having an ego. The old me dies a little bit more every day, and as it does, the more new I become! Of course, quarterbacks are more prone to have a gigantic ego because they score most of the touchdowns.

Fans keep score; they don't keep track of defensive stands! Running backs score a lot of touchdowns too! They tend to get cocky as well. We all get cocky from time to time is my point.

No man has ever been or will ever be as humble as Jesus! That is who we should all look up to! It is extremely hard to be shining bright for Christ, and shining so bright that everyone sees; and to remain humble enough to allow the light to keep on shining.

When we live for Christ, day in and day out, we definitely shine! Whether people who see us are Christians or Buddhist or straight up Atheists, they all notice our peace and love that we pass onto others.

Sometimes, we are shining and don't even know how bright we actually appear to others. If we allow our heads to boil up too big, then we are only dimming the light God has entrusted us. God's light is pure. He didn't call us to carry it perversely. He has called us to shine bright for Him, and recognize the light is ALL about Him. When Jesus rode on a donkey into town, even the donkey knew the palms laid out before them weren't for him. God expects us to at least be as wise as the donkey he rode on. This means we must understand we are stewards of God's Kingdom. A misconception of what this Christian walk is all about could lead to destruction like it did for our adversary, the devil. Pride falls before destruction. Don't allow your ego to be larger than your call.

In Matthew 25, Jesus tells us "the parable of the talents." Talents can be perceived as an actual God given talent or simply money that we are given. Either way, the One who provides the talents is going to observe how the talents are used. Whatever is done in the dark will be brought to light. If you are a deacon at the church on Sundays but hanging out at the strip clubs on Saturdays, you can't be trusted with money. You can't be a deacon anymore. If you get away with it for a season, that season of staying hid will run into another season of it being exposed.

On the contrary, if you invest $20 every week into a local ministry that helps feed the homeless, you will reap a harvest of the seeds sown in due season. God loves a cheerful giver.

""Again, the Kingdom of Heaven can be illustrated by the story of a man going on a long trip. He called together his servants and entrusted his money to them while he was gone. He gave five bags of silver to one, two bags of silver to another, and one bag of silver to the last—dividing it in proportion to their abilities. He then left on his trip. "The servant who received the five bags of silver began to invest the money and earned five more. The servant with two bags of silver also went to work and earned two more. But the servant who received the one bag of silver dug a hole in the ground and hid the master's money. "After a long time their master returned from his trip and called them to give an account of how they had used his money. The servant to whom he had entrusted the five bags of silver came forward with five more and said, 'Master, you gave me five bags of silver to invest, and I have earned five more.' "The master was full of praise. 'Well done, my good and faithful servant. You have been faithful in handling this small amount, so now I will give you many more responsibilities. Let's celebrate together! ' "The servant who had received the two bags of silver came forward and said, 'Master, you gave me two bags of silver to invest, and I have earned two more.' "The master said, 'Well done, my good and faithful servant. You have been faithful in handling this small amount, so now I will give you many more responsibilities. Let's celebrate together!'"

~ Matthew 25:14-23 (NLT)

So, notice that every believer is given a ministry to carry out and the Lord observes how they do. Higher callings, which requires much responsibility, are given to those who are faithful.

Faith the size of a mustard seed is tremendously rewarded! Those who are regarded as faithful by God are entrusted with much. Those who aren't faithful won't be entrusted with much. When we use what God gives us to give Him glory, we demonstrate the faithfulness of a mind that's been renewed. The mission is to use the blessings of God for His glory. It is not about being successful, but it is about being faithful! When we faithfully tithe to a ministry or a church of our choice every month, we allow our funds to be further blessed, and our incoming funds either grow or our necessary expenses decrease.

Sometimes our income grows while our expenses decline too. When were faithful in the small things consistently, we will soon be entrusted with more. Ask yourself, "Am I giving God glory by my stewardship? Am I being faithful with what God's giving me? Am I humble with the talents and gifts God has given me **OR** am I using my gifts and talents to exalt myself and feed my pride?

""Then the servant with the one bag of silver came and said, 'Master, I knew you were a harsh man, harvesting crops you didn't plant and gathering crops you didn't cultivate. I was afraid I would lose your money, so I hid it in the earth. Look, here is your money back.' "But the master replied, 'You wicked and lazy servant! If you knew I harvested crops I didn't plant and gathered crops I didn't cultivate, why didn't you deposit my money in the bank? At least I could have gotten some interest on it.' "Then he ordered, 'Take the money from this servant, and give it to the one with the ten bags of silver. To those who use well what they are given, even more will be given, and they will have an abundance. But from those who do nothing, even what little they have will be taken away. Now throw this useless servant into outer darkness, where there will be weeping and gnashing of teeth.'"

~ **Matthew 25:24-30 (NLT)**

It is best we understand that when we hang onto the blessings God gives us without allowing it to be put to Kingdom use for His glory, we are robbing God and destroying ourselves. When we take ownership of the things He gives to us, we are being prideful rather than humble. Pride comes before the fall. When God gives blessings, He has purpose behind it. If we miss the purpose, we miss God. When we miss God, we miss the blessing, and forfeit all possibilities. It is quite obvious that when God gives us a blessing, He expects us to not take it for granted, but to put it to good use instead. God has anointed me as a Minister for Him, with gifts of teaching, counseling, preaching, and writing. So, if I decide to just go and hide out in the Bahamas, fail to fulfill God's call on my life, and neglect the gifts He's given me; I would be quenching the flow of God's Spirit in my life! Why should I quench God's Spirit and wound other's from receiving what God has for them through me?

That's why it's so important we fulfill God's purpose and not miss out on what God's doing. There are too many people that just want to form their own beliefs and hide from the truth. The truth is real!

"I am the way, the truth, and the life. No one comes to the Father except through Me."

~John 14:6

He hasn't called us to run from Him and bury our gifts. Instead, He's called us to come unto Him with childlike faith and become empowered by His grace to become ambassadors for Him!

"I am the true grapevine, and my Father is the gardener. He cuts off every branch of mine that doesn't produce fruit, and he prunes the branches that do bear fruit so they will produce even more... Yes, I am the vine; you are the branches. Those who remain in me, and I in them, will produce much fruit. For apart from me you can do nothing."

~ John 15:1-2,5

In other words, just like Matthew 25 says... We are given talents that are meant to benefit the Kingdom and when we don't use those talents for the right reasons, we hurt ourselves by quenching the Spirit of God's work in our lives. However, when we recognize the gifts we have while understanding His purposes for us using them, we have the direction we need.

Then, it's up to each person to follow The Lord's direction while maturing in humility. Humility is necessary for growth. A prideful person with an arrogant attitude can't mature in Christ until repentance takes place. You may be a piano player called to play in a Gospel band that causes thousands to surrender to Christ. If you don't play the piano in the band you are meant to play in; those thousands of people don't get reached how they are supposed to.

This hinders the Kingdom, so why should there not be a hindrance in your own life? If I commit a crime, I am going to have to pay some consequences! If I donate 35% of the proceeds from this book to multiple ministries, then I will still be more than blessed than I deserve. I am writing this book because God has given me the talent to do so and I am not going to get lazy and neglect my responsibility as an ambassador of God. I pray that each and every one of you that read this book have a spiritual awakening and have a better understanding of who our beloved Savior is. I can't allow a wave to carry me to shore when I fight it. If I get caught up in a rip tide, my best bet of survival is to go with flow and allow the tide to carry me in. If I don't, I die. The same goes for living our daily lives. If we continue to struggle with God and fight against Him, our lives only become more complicated. It is after we fully surrender to God and abide by His ways and principles of life that we find peace, joy, and contentment.

"If you do whatever I command you, and walk in my ways by keeping my statutes and commands... I'll be with you"

~ 1 Kings 11:38 (NLT)

When our beloved Father is with us, we are protected. When we are with God, we are in His divine favor. When we walk out of God's will, we are no longer under that same spiritual umbrella that has been keeping us safe. When we have God's favor, we end up having people's favor as well. When we have all this favor, life is on our side and more things go right than we ever could have imagined. This doesn't mean we won't face obstacles. That goes with the call. However, it's best to fight the obstacles of life with God on your side. This is far better than living for the world and fighting God.

"Live in harmony with each other. Don't be too proud to enjoy the company of ordinary people. And don't think you know it all!"

~ Romans 12:16 (NLT)

In other words, rather than holding our nose up to the poor and bowing down to the rich, we should treat all mankind the same without any regards to their social or financial status. We shouldn't hold our noses up to anybody. Also, we should never bow to any man instead of God. The right way to treat everybody is, in my opinion, what John 13:34 says: "I have a new command for you. Love each other as I have loved you."

Therefore, a great way to love others in a Christ-like manner is to serve them in a hospitable manner. We don't ever need to feel like we are above any other man because we are not. Even when I am in authority, I am not above the men I lead just because I am their authority. I am their servant. It's almost like I am below them because I am their servant. All men have equal opportunities in life per say. However, some men are better stewards of these opportunities than others. Many of us are very blessed by the Lord.

Our blessings are there for us to be instrumental in blessing others. I would really like to become so blessed that I give away more than I ever allow myself to have. I would love for that to happen with everyone. How much better would the world be then? The problem is not everybody can use the talents or money given to them responsibly. We all must work our way up to the point where we can give a solid portion of what we receive from The Lord while trusting in Jehovah Jireh to re-supply.

"But He gives more grace. Wherefore He said, God resists the proud, but gives grace unto the humble."

~ James 4:6

When I came to Mercy House Ministries and enrolled as a student in Hurley, Mississippi; I was moved by how humbling of an experience that was for me. I always thought of myself as a traveling man that dined in palaces and had drunken wine with kings and queens.

Before I ever made it to the Teen Challenge affiliated program, I went through jail first. By the time I got out of jail, I ate a large Little Caesars pizza, listened to some music and talked with my parents for a while about my life. I cried so hard and so freely! It was such a release. I had finally spoken into existence the forgiveness I had for myself. I couldn't ever seem to forgive myself or repent after my first line of cocaine. After that, I was "toast." For a long time too! Nearly 10 years I was usually drunk, high on marijuana, and strung out on cocaine. For a portion of that I was strung out shooting up heroin too. After I got bailed out of jail by my parents, I was humbling myself by leaving behind all "considered" assets I had at the time.

Now, I have gained so much throughout life. I am successful. I am blessed. I have a loving family. My family is the biggest asset in my life other than Christ, Who is the light of my salvation and the love of my life. Another asset of mine is the men I work with on a daily basis, while in full time ministry, and reaping harvests of their transformation. I love having people in life who look up to me now because of what Christ has done in my life. God is no respecter of persons. He will also do the same for you. All He needs is your permission, submission, and cooperation! God calls us to become expressions of His love. He calls us to resemble Him. He calls us to steward His light productively and influentially. The road of Christian maturity begins with humility.

When I had arrived to the Mercy House, the building definitely needed some work, and still does. The water that is hooked up to the showers and water fountains has a good bit of sulfur running through there. So, the water stinks and the place isn't exactly the Ritz. Oh well!

It humbled me. I was used to Malibu rehabs that had infinity pools and personal masseuses on hand at all times. They had private cooks that could cook a fantastic meal. It was ridiculous! But, now I appreciate the humbling experience.

Sovereignty of Christ

Through all the humility I found Grace. I found a Grace that is sufficient and infinite enough to propel me through life cheerfully with hope, joy, and peace. The key point here is that I never experienced grace until I practiced humility. The humility I practiced was rather pushed on to me, but I am so thankful it was because now I live everyday vicariously through God's grace.

Don't be proud in such a way that is dangerous. Live with love, and trust in God. Serve others cheerfully and with hospitality. The service you then provide will never let you down.

There may be some unhappy campers, but let's get real; there always are. But, when we serve others with the right motives, His light will shine bright. Through humility, we are better stewards of our Heavenly citizenship, and this enhances people's lives! Live a life you can take pride in! If you can take pride in it, there is something valuable there.

Living a life for Christ is a life worth taking pride in. As long as we don't boast about ourselves, but boast in The Lord because of what He has done in our lives, we are showing humility. We will indeed be rewarded for it. God's grace will pile up on us even more as we continue to grow in the level of humility we demonstrate. God's grace is something we need to pile into our lives! If it weren't for God's grace, I would have never had the capability to forgive myself and start over.

I am very thankful for what God has done in my life. I have a life because I left my own behind. I stopped dying and started living! Thank you Jesus!

CHAPTER 4:
We Reap What We Sow

My grandpa, Johnny Earl Ford, decided to build a pond on our land in Meridian, MS several years back. He decided he wanted to have a pond so he could catch catfish out of it with his grandkids. In order for that to happen, he had to first stock the pond with catfish. My grandpa put so many catfish in that pond I believe they had limited space to swim. The recommended number of fish to put in was from 400-600 and he had 1000 put in there! He sure was a character, but I loved him to death and still do. He knew that for him to catch catfish out of a pond he had to first put some in there and let them grow to become good eating size. This is based off a biblical principle known as, "We reap what we sow."

The majority of the people in the world today are aware that the more they give, the more that will come back to them. However, most people refer to that as "Kharma," which is a Buddhist principle. The idea of "Kharma" is a counterfeit of the real thing. God has implemented into this universe the law of "sowing and reaping." Unfortunately, many people are fooled into worshipping Buddha because they agree with the whole idea of Kharma. What many are unaware of is that sowing and reaping had already been established long before Buddha's mother ever knew she was pregnant. It is Jesus, the Living God, who established this principle at the beginning of time.

The Word of God tells us in Galatians 6:7:

> **"Don't be misled – you cannot mock the justice of God. You will always harvest what you plant."**

Another powerful Scripture dealing with this is Matthew 25:14-28 where it is revealed to us that when we steward well what we have been given, we are entrusted with more. Also, if we fail to be a good steward of what's been given, we are no longer trusted. With stewardship of God's Kingdom, we must sow into His glory what's already been given to us. When we use what's been given to us for glorifying God, we will be entrusted with more. In the abundance of what we reap, we are to continue sowing into the glory of God with our time, talents, and treasures.

"Again, the Kingdom of Heaven can be illustrated by the story of a man going on a long trip. He called together his servants and entrusted his money to them while he was gone."

~ Matthew 25:14 (NLT)

If I go on a long trip to leave a farm behind, I will make sure to leave people there to watch over it whom I feel I can trust. My prayer would be that they follow The Lord's direction and capitalize on Kingdom opportunities by handling them in such a way that glorifies God.

"He gave five bags of silver to one, two bags of silver to another, and one bag of silver to the last dividing it in proportion to their abilities. He then left on his trip."

~Matthew 25:15 (NLT)

Some men I would be more comfortable with giving more to because of their abilities. There would be others I would be more comfortable with giving less responsibility to because of their maturity level.

"The servant who received the five bags of silver began to invest the money and earned five more."

~ Matthew 25:16 (NLT)

This particular servant had interest in pleasing his master. Therefore, he actively became involved in putting forth the effort to see his master go home with more than that was entrusted to him. Ideally, a landowner would greatly appreciate an overseer that does more than simply watch over the property.

Those who watch over the property with a purpose to increase its yield are those who will be more trusted. The master would be able to bless those he trusts. He would be skeptical to allow around him those he cannot trust.

"The servant with two bags of silver also went to work and earned two more."

~Matthew 25:17 (NLT)

Regardless of the amount, the principle involves being a good steward who is trustworthy due to faithful, purposeful works. This servant took the two bags of silver that was given to him and went to work to earn more. When The Lord gives you a house to use for ministry, will you get to work and sow into God's glory with that one house? Will you be a good steward of the people that house was given to you for? Will your stewardship cause God to say, "Well done my good and faithful servant. Here's you another house I entrust to you for the purpose of ministering to more souls!"

"But the servant who received the one bag of silver dug a hole in the ground and hid the master's money."

~Matthew 25:18 (NLT)

Hiding money will never make it multiply just like watching over a property without watering the crops doesn't help the property flourish. This servant sowed into the ground instead of the glory of God. When we sow into the things of the world, The Lord has no accumulated interest in giving to us more. But, when we are focused on being good stewards of everything He gives to us, and our purpose is to utilize for His glory; we become trusted servants who have done well. When God can trust you with one house, He will give you another. When God can trust you with one unbeliever, He will send you another. When God can trust you to tithe a monthly income of $1500, He will bless you with $2000 income you can tithe from. When God can trust you with a Sunday school class, He will trust you with a congregation to preach to. When God can trust you with one son or daughter, He is liable to bless you with another.

"After a long time their master returned from his trip and called them to give an account of how they had used his money."

~Matthew 25:19 (NLT)

There comes a time when all things come to light whether good or bad. At some point, we will have to give an answer to our Creator for everything we have ever received. We will also have to give an account to our Lord Jesus Christ for every word we have ever spoken, every dollar we have ever given, and every mission we have ever sown into.

"The servant to whom he had entrusted the five bags of silver came forward with five more and said, 'Master, you gave me five bags of silver to invest, and I have earned five more."

~ Matthew 25:20 (NLT)

Faithful work always produces benefit.

"The master was full of praise. 'Well done, my good and faithful servant. You have been faithful in handling this small amount, so now I will give you many more responsibilities. Let's celebrate together."

~Matthew 25:21 (NLT)

When we handle a little bit wisely, we are entrusted with more.

"The servant who had received the two bags of silver came forward and said, 'Master, you gave me two bags of silver to invest, and I have earned two more."

~Matthew 25:22 (NLT)

"The master said, 'Well done, my good and faithful servant. You have been faithful in handling this small amount, so now I will give you many more responsibilities. Let's celebrate together."

~Matthew 25:23 (NLT)

God celebrates our faithfulness! When we sow into His glory with what's been entrusted to us, we get to share in His glory with Him. Faithful workers get to share with God the fruits of their labor.

"Then the servant with the one bag of silver came and said, 'Master, I knew you were a harsh man, harvesting crops you didn't plant and gathering crops you didn't cultivate."

~Matthew 25:24 (NLT)

This verse constitutes a man simply lying about what his Lord did because he reaped what he sowed. He was lazy with what was given, so he received a lousy return. He sowed into earth rather than sowed into Heaven. He sowed into the world instead of sowing into the glory of God's Kingdom. This servant opposed himself but shifted blame on to his master.

"I was afraid I would lose your money, so I hid it in the earth. Look, here is your money back."

~Matthew 25:25 (NLT)

God is not looking for us to hold on to what He gives us. The purpose of receiving more is meant for extra giving. The purpose of reaping is to continue sowing. Fear is the opposite of faith. This servant was afraid of sowing because he was afraid of losing what was given to him. If he would have been faithful with what was given to him, he would have reaped a harvest of what faithfulness is capable of accomplishing.

"But the master replied, 'You wicked and lazy servant! If you knew I harvested crops I didn't plant and gathered crops I didn't cultivate, why didn't you deposit my money in the bank? At least I could have gotten some interest on it."

~Matthew 25:26-27 (NLT)

This means that the servant should have invested the money so The Lord could have received more when He came to collect. When we receive a blessing from The Lord, there's greater purpose in multiplying it rather than hoarding it. With our lives even, we're called to sow it into Kingdom use so that our lives become an offering unto our Master and Lord, Jesus Christ.

We are to lay our lives down for our brothers, offering our bodies as a sacrifice unto The Lord that is pleasing to Him.

"Then he ordered, 'Take the money from this servant, and give it to the one with the ten bags of silver."

~Matthew 25:28 (NLT)

Whatever is stored up for the wicked may very well fall into the hands of the godly. It doesn't always seem that way.

"A good person leaves an inheritance for their children's children, but a sinners wealth is stored up for the righteous."

~ Proverbs 13:22

God rewards those who are faithful. God blesses faith. Faith pleases God. Faith is what makes us right with God. When we have faith in the works of Jesus and the blood He shed for our sins, we are made righteous. When we utilize what God has given to us well, we earn more. If we sow into the world, we reap from the world it's corruption. When we sow into the flesh we reap from the flesh it's corruption. But, when we sow into pleasing the Spirit, we reap from the Spirit a harvest of everlasting life.

"To those who use well what they are given, even more will be given, and they will have an abundance. But from those who do nothing, even what little they have will be taken away. Now throw this useless servant into outer darkness, where there will be weeping and gnashing of teeth."

~Matthew 25:29-30 (NLT)

We are called to be effective servants. Not slothful. The master sowed money to three servants. The two faithful servants invested the money so their master could reap more than what was first given. But, the one wicked and slothful servant did not. Instead, he buried the money so it would not be lost. He lacked faith, and lost his masters trust. The master sowed and reaped. And, his servants sowed what was given to them so they could reap a reward for their Master. The two servants who were faithful in doing so received a reward. They invested the money faithfully, and were rewarded for it. They became blessed because of their faith. The servant that did not trust the idea of a faithful investment, lost what he was first given.

If we do not invest the gifts God gives us, we hinder the overflow of those gifts. For the gifts and calling of God are irrevocable, meaning without repentance. Romans 11:29 says, "For God's gift and call can never be withdrawn." Therefore, how we use the gifts God has given us can either cause an increase or decrease. We won't lose our gifts but to bury them is to wound others from receiving what God has to give them through you. God gave me the gift to write and I hadn't written for a while, so I figured I better go ahead and get back to

51

writing before I'm too rusty to start back. He gave me the gift to write, speak, and converse with people kindly. The hardest ones to keep active are speaking and writing. The reason for this is simply because I don't always have the opportunity to speak in a pulpit, and it's hard to find time to write.

I thoroughly enjoy writing because all I have to stare at is a computer screen rather than several hundred people on the edge of their seat anxious to hear what I have to say. I hadn't spoken for a while not too long ago. So I was nervous for my next speaking engagement. I prepared myself and I spoke so much better than usual it was ridiculous! But, we must remember that it is all because of a gift that has been given to me by a power greater than myself. That power is God, The Almighty. Jesus Christ made it all possible by His heroic actions from the day of His birth until the day He was crucified and rose from the dead, giving us hope for a better life and a life of eternity. It is so amazing how bad life is here on earth compared to the life we are granted when we pass over into Heaven.

The New Jerusalem puts this old earth to shame, and that is saying a lot considering how wonderful life on earth really can be. It hasn't always been like that for me down here but ever since I met Jesus it has been a life I am in love with! I give God praise for my relationship with Him every day! I am in love with the majestic wonder and beauty of Christ's work He has incorporated into my life. I love watching Him incorporate His mighty works and answers to prayer in other people's lives so much too! God is awesome. He really is. I have a giant prayer list I pray over for a while and pretty soon I begin crossing them off and replacing them with new ones because the old prayers have been answered. Cancer gets healed. Attitudes change. Relationships get mended. People's land heals. Lives turn around for the better. The guilty are proven innocent because of the change the judge sees. The impossible turns into a grand achievement. People are beautiful creatures. We have dominion over plants where artistically made gardens are beautifully constructed because of that dominion we have. We have dominion over animals where we train some of the wildest animals to do some of the most amazing things. Another great Scripture that pertains to sowing and reaping is that of Galatians 6:7,8:

"Be not deceived; God is not mocked: for whatsoever a man sows, that shall he also reap. For he who sows to his flesh shall of the flesh reap corruption; but he who sows to the Spirit shall of the Spirit reap life everlasting."

~ Galatians 6:7,8

Believers can sometimes be deceived. Therefore, those who do not yet believe may be easily misled. God is mocked when we put Him second or third. He is honored when we put Him first. The law of sowing and reaping has been incorporated into the unseen principalities of the universe. We shall receive from that in which we sow. If we sow tomatoes we will receive more tomatoes. If we sow money, we shall receive money. If we pour our lives into others, then others will pour their lives into us. The law of sowing and reaping will never fail. Therefore, do not be discouraged if you have been sowing for a long time but have not yet reaped. Your time is due to reap a harvest very soon.

"And let us not get tired of doing what is right for after a while we will reap a harvest of blessings if we do not get discouraged and give up."

~Galatians 6:9 (TLB)

Take notice, verse 9 follows 7 and 8. There is a reason for that. I can do what is right for 10 years and feel weary because the work may not seem to have paid off yet, but I should understand that my harvest is only around the corner. If I give up because I get tired and discouraged, then I will indeed miss out on the harvest of blessings. When we sow with what Christ has given us we will receive more from Christ. When I gave drugs out to other people it only fed into my corruption deeper by getting me more involved in the dark world of drug dealing. When I pour my heart into other men's lives who are battling addiction, it ensures the deliverance I have already attained, which comes from God. That's why it says, **"For he who sows to his flesh shall of the flesh reap corruption."**

If we live for ourselves, our brothers and sisters will be robbed and suffer because of it. But, when we live for others many benefit because of it. It is impossible to sow in the flesh and reap in the spirit. It is also impossible to reap without sowing. For crops to grow, they must be planted. For those of us that give full expression to living for Him by doing good every time an opportunity presents itself, we make it known that we are on His side. We are called to become transformed into expressions of God's love.

A man that works is due a check.

"Give generously to them and do so without a grudging heart; then because of this the LORD your God will bless you in all your work and in everything you put your hand to."

~Deuteronomy 15:10 (NIV)

If we are going to do anything for anyone we ought to do things for others with generosity. It's very rewarding when we do. It is so rewarding that we are guaranteed a thirty, or sixty, or one hundred fold. This comes out of Mark 4, where Jesus talks about the "sower of the seed."

"Listen! A farmer went out to plant some seed. As he scattered it across his field, some of the seed fell on a footpath, and the birds came and ate it. Other seed fell on shallow soil with underlying rock. The seed sprouted quickly because the soil was shallow. But the plant soon wilted under the hot sun, and since it didn't have deep roots, it died. Other seed fell among thorns that grew up and choked out the tender plants so they produced no grain. Still other

seeds fell on fertile soil, and they sprouted, grew, and produced a crop that was thirty, sixty, and even a hundred times as much as had been planted!" Then he said, "Anyone with ears to hear should listen and understand."

~ Mark 4:3-9 (NLT)

As we sow into others the Good News, we must always be aware of this Scripture and what it means. Not everyone that we minister to will hear the Gospel and carry it throughout the rest of their lives. Some will hear it but not listen to it. Some will listen to it and live by it for a little while. But, eventually they will stop and go back to their old ways. Others hear it, listen to it, and live by it for as long as they can.

This happens until the world robs them for all they have heard pressing them to be conformed to the world's ways. Some hear the Word and live for God forever because they have faith that what they have heard is true, and they understand how to apply it to their lives. These hearers pay attention to what they hear and produce much fruit; some thirty, some sixty, and some even a hundred fold!

And do not be conformed to this world, but be transformed by the renewing of your mind, that you may prove what is that good and acceptable and perfect will of God.

~Romans 12:2 (NKJV)

The best way to be in His will is by being in the center of His Word.

There are 1,189 chapters in the Bible.

There are 594 chapters before Psalm 118 and there are 594 chapters after. The longest chapter is Psalm 119 and the shortest is Psalm 117. The chapter in-between is Psalm 118 and believe it or not, the center verse of the Bible is verse 8 of Psalm 118; which tells us that **"it is better to trust in The Lord than to put confidence in man."** One version says, **"Better to take refuge in The Lord than to put confidence in princes."**

It is easy for us to want to put a great deal of confidence in the preacher because he carries the message. However, it is best for us to investigate the Message by directly going to God's Word and finding it out for ourselves. With me, personally, I don't put much confidence in myself. I put all my confidence in God because through Him, I may do all things (Philippians 4:13). When it is just me I am not even a speck of this whole universe, but with His authority I tell my problems to go away. With the...

"faith of a mustard seed we may tell our mountains to move."

~Matthew 17:20

I enjoy planting the Message into the ears of all living creatures. I love being spontaneous enough to tell my strangers how much Jesus loves them. I want people to understand Jesus as their supernatural hero Who suffered in the natural for them to become free! He died a horrific death that none of us can even fathom!

I like to tell people about the character of Christ. Unfortunately, many see Him as a timid, weak man when He was really the baddest dude that ever walked the planet! He got nailed to a tree and bled for 6 hours straight! Some of us can't even hardly bear road trips for 5 hours with family.

When it comes to all the parables and stories Jesus told, they had such great meaning it blows my mind! I was telling somebody the other day how I fell in love with the way Johnny Depp played George Jung in the movie "Blow." Johnny Depp said, "Sorry I could not get you the $75K, so I brought you $100K instead!" I used to love the glamorous styles of conversation I referred to as gangster realness. I loved then what I thought "real" was. As that was the lifestyle I used to live, it was also the language I spoke. But, then I met Jesus and discovered how "real" His character was while on earth. I found it hard not to acknowledge Him as the truth itself. I came to an understanding that everything He ever has spoken or will ever speak is 100% truth. He explains "greatness" to us by calling a little child over to Him and teaching to us what it means to have "child-like faith."

We are filthy rags but with Jesus we are righteous. Through our faith in believing that Jesus died on the Cross for our sins so we may be forgiven, we are righteous in God's eyes.

When Paul wrote to the Philippians, he told them that they were the only ones who gave him financial help when he first brought the Good News before traveling to Macedonia (Philippians 4:15). The Philippians, in fact, helped Paul more than once in their financial giving. Why not give to a man that is bringing something of great value? It is only fair to pay a man for his work, especially when that man is providing information on our Lord, Savior, and Creator.

The Philippians provided what they could, financially, so that Paul and his ministry would be able to go further on. We get rewarded for our sowing by reaping a harvest of blessings.

"This same God who takes care of me will supply all your needs from his glorious riches, which have been given to us in Christ Jesus."

~ Philippians 4:19

Paul is telling them that the same God who has taken care of him will supply all their needs from His glorious riches as well! As these Philippians sowed into the ministry God was carrying through Paul, they would reap a harvest because of their giving. This God is Jesus Christ Himself whom died on the Cross for us as a sacrifice and rose from the dead to give us hope for a better life; a new life; and eternal life! God has dominion over the entire universe! Therefore, when we have access to what He has dominion over, we tap into receiving what we need after first giving to others their needs.

"When we sow into the Spirit, we reap from the Spirit."

~Galatians 6:8

When I tithe into a church, which is the House of God, I receive blessings from Heaven. My finances end up blessed. When I share what I have by providing for others what they need, I end up receiving more than what I need because God expects me to continue providing for others. He gives to me in proportion to my giving, and also according to His expectations. God has expectations placed on us all with our stewarding over finances. The better we handle a little, the sooner we become entrusted with more. If God can get extra finances "through you," He will be sure to get it to you. God loves a cheerful giver!

As we sow into each other's lives the shared revelations of Christ as brothers and sisters in God's Kingdom, we receive an even better perception of His character. This is because of the law of sowing and reaping. Have you ever gone to a Bible study and walked away with less understanding than what you first went it with? If you have, you may need to find a new Bible study group. When we go into a Bible study with something to share, others usually do the same, and we are able to walk away with more understanding than we first had.

The more sodas I give away, the more I end up receiving. The other day I had to pick up a man that I am probably related to up in Meridian at 3:00 in the morning to bring back down to Mercy House to change his life. I did not have any money on my debit card but I had $100 stashed away in my shoebox for a rainy day. I took a friend with me and we picked this guy up. I bought gas, bought energy drinks, then bought us all food which costs $50 total. That same day, I received a check from my Mimi for $50 exactly. So, because I spent the money faithfully I not only was able to pick up a man that was near death, but also ended up reaping what I had sowed.

God is phenomenally awesome! Is He NOT!??

Check it out everyone! When you treat people with the love of Christ and share with them the Good News, you will not necessarily reach every person the way you would like, but for some people you will. As long as you keep sharing the love of Christ with others, you will not fail. As a result, some people will be transformed and do the same thing you did to them, to others. Some people will flip you off and tell you to go away. Some people will just listen and you may never see them again. Either way, as long as you don't get discouraged and quit, you will be blessed by harvests of blessings season after season!

His love never fails. It will never give up. So why should we?

"WE ARE ALL CITIZENS OF HEAVEN ONCE WE HAVE ACCEPTED CHRIST AS OUR LORD AND SAVIOR. THAT'S WHY IT'S IMPORTANT TO RESEMBLE 'WHOSE' WE ARE."

~TY FORD

CHAPTER 5:
Bearing Fruit

There are trees that produce leaves. There are plants that produce vegetables. There are also trees and plants that produce fruit. Some fruit tastes sweet off some trees and some fruit tastes bitter off others. We, as humans, all bear fruit. Some of us bear bad fruit and others good.

What kind of fruit do you wish to bear? Sweet fruit comes from trees and plants that have been well taken care of. On another note, bitter fruit comes from those that have not been taken well care of. What good is a tree that has bad fruit? Matthew 21:19 tells us that Jesus cursed a fig tree after He saw there was nothing being produced. The fig tree was in season to produce, yet fruitless.

"And seeing a fig tree by the wayside, he went to it and found nothing on it but only leaves. And he said to it, 'May no fruit ever come from you again!' And the fig tree withered at once."

~Matthew 21:19

Why didn't that fig tree bear figs like it should have? Well, why do some people not bear good fruit? That's easy! They don't have Jesus in their life. They have not given Jesus permission to rule their life. They have not submitted to Jesus. They are still living in sin. They have clung to their own life, which profits the Kingdom little to nothing. They have not been good stewards of the gifts and talents The Lord has given them. Just like Israel had opportunity after opportunity to get things right; some people have had many opportunities as well but just don't get it! When we rebel against Christ and His commands for us, we curse ourselves.

God wants to use us, and He wants to bear His life giving fruit through us all! Those who have given up their lives in order to follow Jesus,

61

allow fruit to flourish from them. Willingness and obedience allows a passage for the Spirit of God to flow through us. Jesus expects to find good fruit from us just like He expected that fig tree to produce figs! When we are connected to Christ through an active and intimate relationship, His fruit flourishes through us. His Word tells us, "Out of the belly shall flow rivers of living water!" These rivers provide the nourishment to grow in us His life bearing fruit. When we are fruitful, others are able to feed on God's Kingdom through us.

What kind of fruit are you trying to produce? Well, the only fruit that is meant for us to produce is that of the Holy Spirit mentioned in Galatians 5:22-23.

"But the Fruit of the Spirit is love, joy, peace, faithfulness, gentleness, kindness, goodness, self-control, and patience. There is no law against these things!"

~ Galatians 5:22-23

This fruit is of the Holy Spirit and not of the world. We must realize that this fruit may only be produced by the Holy Spirit. We must open ourselves up to God with a willingness to be used, in order to develop a heart for obedience. Why be open?

Well, if we close our minds at all then we are not yielding to God's power, thoughts, and ways. If we shut out God, we miss His love, joy, and peace. But, when we are open to God, we become mesmerized and amazed by His thoughts and also His ways. "His thoughts are higher than ours just as His ways are too" (Isaiah 55:8,9 paraphrase).

The effectiveness of our obedience will be a reflection of our relationship with Christ. Our fruitfulness is determined by our obedience. Our obedience springs from our relationship. Our relationship starts with an openness to His Spirit, and the willingness for intimacy with Him as our Lord. God wants to move in your life because He was in love with you before your greatest fall and before your greatest climb. He not only wants to use you. He wants to restore your soul from a place of brokenness, and into the dimension of wholeness He has for you.

When I was still in the program at Mercy House, I had a pass that ended up being a significant day for me! My dad picked me up and it was around my birthday. He surprised me by telling me he brought our boat down just so we could go fishing. I was stoked to hear that! He also surprised me with a cross that he bought from some Teen Challenge women in a whole other state!

We went to Whataburger to eat and ordered our food just like any other normal day. The man that took our order had me thinking about how honorable he must be. A man that is obviously dealing with pain that he covers up. He was working a regular job with average responsibilities. I noticed he had to wear a hair net, which had me thinking how humble he must be. When I was living for the world and selling drugs, I would have never worked a job that would have required me to wear a hair net. This was because I was prideful, arrogant, and corrupt to the point where I chose to sell drugs rather than uphold a regular job that would require such humility from me. Compassion struck my heart for this young man.

God told me to give the cross to him and tell him a little bit about my past along with what the crucifixion and resurrection of Jesus Christ had done for me. It was placed on my heart to tell this young man how much Jesus had changed my life. I was meant to do this and I couldn't allow myself to shrink back in fear because of a full restaurant. I told my dad what was on my mind and my heart. I asked him what he thought I should do. He said, "Well son, if God is leading you to do something then you better do it because you can't go wrong doing right." I said, "Well alright Pops. Go grab the cross out of the truck then." So he did. I got it. I said a prayer. Then, delivered the cross to the young man just after he had brought a tray out to some customers. I told him that the cross stood for Who had changed my life completely. I told him about my past with drug use and how much different I had become ever since knowing Christ. I told him that even if things were going alright for him in life, Jesus is still the way to so much more. I also told him that if things were bad, Jesus would meet him in his mess and turn things around for the good.

It's all about Jesus Christ! He died on the cross for us so we could have right standing with our Father, and a life everlasting with Him! He got beaten so brutally that it costs Him a whole lot of pain and suffering for us to have free access to salvation through the cross! The cross is the most meaningful symbol of life. It represents the "conquering of death," and "gateway to life."

Through openness, I was able to respond to God's lead. Through His obedience to the Father, I have been inspired to serve God obediently as well. I must say that this was only the introduction to my active participation in obeying God's call on my life. I felt like a "Child of the One true King" and what a spiritual high it was!

"Wherefore by their fruits you shall know them."

                                          ~ Matthew 7:20

Before verse 20, Scripture speaks of good trees and bad trees. "Beware of false prophets" is the subtitle,

"Beware of false prophets, who come to you in sheep's clothing but inwardly are ravenous wolves. You will recognize them by their fruits. Are grapes gathered from thorn-bushes, or figs from thistles?" So, every healthy tree bears good fruit, but the diseased tree bears bad fruit. A healthy tree cannot bear bad fruit, nor can a diseased tree bear good fruit. Every tree that does not bear good fruit is cut down and thrown into the fire. There have been, there are, and there will be even more "false prophets."

                                          ~ Matthew 7:15-19

They pose as Christians just so they can be seen as credible and reliable with their faulty information. They twist the truth just enough to change it and not enough to be always noticed. That's why 2 Timothy 2:15 tells us to "be a good steward so that we may rightly divide the word of truth." The better we know the Word, the harder it will be for us to become deceived. The fruit from false prophets will not produce good fruit in others. There will usually be division or strife as a result. To love Christ is righteousness and to love self is evil. To love Christ in our self is one thing, but to be self-righteous is not of Christ.

The best tree is a tree whose roots are deeply rooted in Jesus Christ. When a person builds there foundation to life by drawing their roots deep in God's love, they are going to be extremely fruitful. The fruits of a person shall reveal their spiritual existence. The fruit one bears resembles where they are at in their spiritual walk. Some may reveal they are devout Christians and others fruit may reveal they are one of the many anti-christ's.

"Oh, the joys of those who do not follow the advice of the wicked, or stand around with sinners, or join in with mockers. But they delight in the law of the Lord, meditating on it day and night. They are like trees planted along the riverbank, bearing fruit each season. Their leaves never wither, and they prosper in all they do."

~ Psalm 1: 1-3

Therefore, those who surround themselves with fellow Christians and meditate on Scripture will be blessed beyond measure! It is wise to have mentors in authority over our lives while also having some under our wing. We must have a "Paul" in our lives and it's great to have a "Timothy" in our lives as well. We must be ministered to, and do some ministering to others as well. By meditating on Scripture, we are saturating ourselves with God's Word. When God's Word is engraved in our hearts and accessible by our minds, we walk then by the Spirit with a crucifixion of our flesh. We must stay connected with the Living Water by constantly hearing the Good News of Christ. When we do this, we bear fruit each and every season. That's what living a resurrected life is all about!

"Faith comes by hearing, and hearing by the Word of God."

~Romans 10:17

The fruit we bear will always be good and acceptable as long as we are living the "perfect will of God" for our lives. We discover what God's perfect will is for our lives by reading, studying, and meditating on God's Word. As branches of the "True Vine," we are engrafted in Christ empowered to endure all storms and faulty weather. In other words, when we bear good fruit there will be trials and storms that will literally challenge the fruit production in our lives.

Our fruit production must be challenged in order for it to truly grow and flourish. Storms serve as catalysts to our spiritual growth. They are necessary in order for our root system to cling that much deeper in Christ. Storms and trials can often times shake our faith. That's why we must lay a firm foundation as we become deeply rooted in Christ. We must develop patient endurance so that we can faithfully embrace the stormy trials. Trials and storms may seem like they are there to destroy us. However, they are really designed to increase our faith and strengthen our character with the disposition of Jesus Christ.

"Blessed are they which are persecuted for Righteousness' sake: for theirs is the Kingdom of Heaven."

~ Matthew 5:10

This refers to the suffering and persecution that our journey of following Christ will encounter. When the facets to our faith are securely fastened in Christ, we have what it takes to overcome all stormy weather because our root system is secure and stable. Our righteousness is made by our faith in Christ and what He did at the

Cross. Christ is our Righteousness and we are God's righteousness because of our faith in Christ!

"He made Him who knew no sin to be sin on our behalf, so that we might become the righteousness of God in Him."

~2 Corinthians 5:21

Our fruit may be challenged in times of persecution. Sufferings will come that shakes our faith. Stand on guard because these moments will come!

"Stand steady and don't be afraid of suffering for The Lord. Bring others to Christ. Leave nothing undone that you ought to do."

~2 Timothy 4:5

When trials come, be joyful! You are in the fire being purified in such a time. We ought to truly seek after the refining of our faith. Purification takes fire, trials, and persecution.

"My dear brothers and sisters, whenever trouble comes your way, let it be an opportunity for joy. For when your faith is tested, your endurance has a chance to grow. So let it grow, for when your endurance is fully developed you will be strong in character and ready for anything."

~ James 1:2-4

Be joyful in trials and persecution because your faith is being tested, giving your endurance the chance to grow. And, once your endurance is fully developed you will receive the deposits of Christ-like character, which will strengthen and empower you! We can't overcome life's obstacles the way we are called to without the deposits of Christ's character in us. In order to be strengthened in His character, we must develop the patient endurance our trials require from us. It is impossible for us to build up endurance without our faith first being tested.

Your faith won't be tested without trouble coming your way. The increasing of your faith requires opposition. In order to be strengthened physically, one must exercise routinely. There must be opposition to ones exercise for that person to grow in their strength. The same is true for one's spiritual growth. Opposition through storms and trials are necessary for our spiritual growth.

So, be joyful when trouble comes your way. Growing in Christ is something to be joyful about!

"If you confess with your mouth that Jesus is Lord and believe in your heart that God raised Him from the dead, you will be *saved*. For it is by believing in your heart that you are made right with God and it is by confessing with your mouth that you are *saved*."

~Romans 10:9,10

Repeat after me... "Jesus, I love you and I thank You for dying such a brutal death on The Cross so I may be forgiven for all of my sins. I accept Your Sacrifice. I confess I have sinned and believe in Your forgiveness. I accept You into my life and commit my life fully to You." We all say, "Amen!"

Now you shall receive the Holy Spirit and will learn how to draw from Him spiritual discernment and understanding.

"When the Spirit of Truth comes, He will guide you into all truth. He will not be presenting His own ideas. He will be telling you what He has heard. He will tell you about the future."

~John 16:13

Become baptized with water immediately by a Man of God or a Woman of God. Do it formally in a church or even informally in a lake with that person of spiritual authority explaining the process to you.

"Then Peter said unto them, Repent, and be baptized every one of you in the Name of Jesus Christ for the Remission of sins and you shall receive the Gift of the Holy Spirit."

~ Acts 2:38, 39

Repentance and Baptism are both crucial to salvation. They are imperative even! To repent is to be thankful for forgiveness of sins and to turn 180 degrees away from the sin and lifestyle it entailed. Turning 180 degrees from sin is forsaking the sin that held you into bondage. Receive the fullness of freedom God has for you by way of repentance. After you accept Christ as your Lord and Savior, take up your cross daily and "Follow Him!" Follow Him with interactive gratitude as you believe what He did at the Cross has been sufficient enough for your forgiveness.

"But if you refuse to take up your cross and follow Me you are not worthy of being Mine. If you cling to your life you will lose it, but if you give it up for Me you will find it!"

~ Matthew 10:38,39

Be worthy of being His by making the commitment to take up your cross every single day and follow Him! Follow Him because you count Him as more than worthy.

"The axe is already laid at the root of the trees; therefore every tree that does not bear good fruit is cut down and thrown into the fire. As for me, I baptize you with water for repentance, but He who is coming after me is mightier than I, and I am not fit to remove His sandals; He will baptize you with the Holy Spirit and fire"

~Matthew 3:10 - 3:11 (NASB)

This is where John the Baptist prepares the way for Christ's coming and ministry. This sums up much of what has been already explained in this chapter so far. Those who produce bad fruit are on their way to Hell until they repent of their sins and follow Jesus. It's important to be baptized with water as it's an outward expression of inward obedience. It signifies that one belongs to Christ and His body. After being baptized with water, the "fire" is uh-coming! Fire stands for trials, persecutions, and storms. Welcome to the Christian lifestyle. Look at Jesus. After He was baptized, He faced the confrontation of the devil. He was baptized with water then thrown in a fiery trial. Welcome to the Walk-A-Thon a Christian endures. It is so adventurous, sweet, and tastes so good it makes you want to Slap Yo Momma! ... Wait, that wouldn't be very Christian like! Just figuratively speaking. You get the point. I have lived an adventurous life all my life, but the Christian walk surpasses any lifestyle I have ever lived!

The Pharisees continually challenged Jesus and His teaching's. They were all so lame thinking they knew it all and were with God and God was with them, but they didn't even recognize Him when He was right in front of their faces. Their fruit was corrupt, but Jesus's fruit was good and everyone who lives for Jesus and loves Him will find themselves producing good fruit as well.

"Either make the tree good, and his fruit good; or else make the tree corrupt, and his fruit corrupt: for the tree is known by his fruit."

~Matthew 12:33

There cannot be a mixture of both good and evil. You either choose Jesus and learn enough about who He is so that you may produce His kind of fruit. Or, you choose living for the world and it's corruption; producing bad fruit. The world is going to Hell in a hand basket. Marijuana is becoming legal and I will be the first to tell you I was all about it becoming legal! But, just because it is legal does not mean it is okay to smoke and/or eat. If the world says it is okay, it is not necessarily "*okay.*" Alcohol is legal and people drink it to the point of doing ungodly acts. It is legal to drive with a .07 alcohol level. This causes people to challenge what they can blow in the alcohol tube after drinking and cruising around in a car. Many folks have killed others because of such so-called 'justified' actions.

Marijuana being legal causes the world to believe it is okay to partake. Alcohol being legal causes the world to believe it is okay to partake. The Bible talks about wine so people justify their drinking. Jesus and His disciples didn't go around drinking wine with gluttony and overindulgence. They drank a glass with dinner. King Herod on the other hand was an evil man that got drunk. Some of us cannot drink because over-indulgence poses to great of a risk. I am one example. It's not that I don't want everybody else to not have fun because I can't. I just want people to have a proper understanding on such a risky topic. Be careful.

"We must be as wary as snakes and as harmless as doves."

~Matthew 10:16

The enemy preys on us like a lion waiting to devour the weak.

"Be sober- minded; be watchful. Your adversary the devil prowls around like a roaring lion, seeking someone to devour. Resist him, firm in your faith, knowing that the same kinds of suffering are being experienced by your brotherhood throughout the world."

~1 Peter 5:8,9

People wonder why I don't simply smoke herb as they claim they don't think God would mind. I am prey for the devil, so if I get high, guess what? I will be more easily deceived into making other bad choices and confusion will pose a mighty threat. The devil is author of confusion and king of deceit. Therefore, I choose to be "sober-minded" as the Bible says in 1 Peter 5:8.

"I Am the True Grapevine, and My Father is the Vine Dresser (Gardener). Every branch in Me that does not bear fruit He takes away: and every branch that bears fruit, He purges it, so that it may bring forth more fruit."

~ John 15:1,2

Jesus is the source of life while the Father is the owner. Every believer who is in Christ (in which one must be in Christ to even be a believer), bears fruit because of the Holy Spirit which is perfectly connected to Christ. If a believer refuses to accept all of God's Word and apply it to their life, they risk being taken away from the goodness of God. Often times, believers that fall away become shaken by God through difficult circumstances so that they will repent and return to God. Those who are already bearing fruit will bear even more fruit because God gives an increase to believers who steward well the faith they were first given. Jesus Christ and what He did at the Cross must become the total Object of one's faith in order for them to produce good fruit through the help of the Holy Spirit.

"Now you are clean through the Word which I have spoken unto you. Abide in Me, and I in you. As the branch cannot bear fruit of itself, except it abide in the Vine; no more can you, except you abide in Me."

~ John 15:3,4

The Word cleans us and renews our mind and renews our Spirit. The Word totally points to the cross and what Christ did there! Recognize what the cross stands for and what all it represents. When we comprehend the cross and accept it, believe in it, and understand it; we allow God to take over our lives.

When God reins from our hearts, our true living has just begun. Good fruit may come from God ONLY! Bad fruit comes from the rejection of Christ. Separation from Christ brings on demolition and destruction.

"Humility precedes honor and haughtiness falls before destruction."

~Proverbs 18:12

"I Am the Vine, you are the branches: he who abides in Me, and I in him, the same brings forth much fruit: for without Me you can do nothing. If a man abide not in Me, he is cast forth as a branch, and is withered; and men gather them, and cast them into the fire, and they are burned."

~ John 15:5, 6

In other words, Christ is the Vine; not the world, not the preacher, not the church, not the boss of your job, not your favorite sports player, but JESUS is the Vine! He is the boss!

"I can do all things through Christ who strengthens me."

~Philippians 4:13

But, I can do nothing without Him. Without recognizing the "Source of Life," we become removed from the "Source" at large!

If faith in Christ at the cross is not obtained, Hell becomes the final destination. God the Father has prepared a wonderful plan that involves good works for every one of us.

"For we are God's workmanship created in Christ Jesus to do good works which God prepared in advance for us to do."

~ Ephesians 2:10

"For God knew His people in advance, and He chose them to become like His Son, so that His Son would be the firstborn among many brothers and sisters."

~ Romans 8:29

73

Sovereignty of Christ

You see, God has called us to become like Him and has given us good works to glorify Him. Unfortunately, some people forfeit their eternal peace of God's plan for their own plan instead. God hasn't predestined anyone's eternity to become Hell. He has predestined greatness for us all. He has a wonderful plan for each and every individual. What determines the course of life is our own free will.

Why do some people go to Hell? Not because God sent them there. But, because they rejected Christ and His plan. That's why it is so important to trust in Christ and not miss the wonderful plan He has for our lives. He calls His disciples sons and daughters.

"You did not choose Me but I chose you, and appointed you that you would go and bear fruit, and that your fruit would remain, so that whatever you ask of the Father in My name He may give to you. This I command you, that you love one another."

~ John 15:16 - 15:17 (NASB)

We have all been designed for a specific ministry bringing things to the table that others cannot. You don't need a 501(c)3 to live out the ministry God has designed you for. It requires no serious paperwork. All you need is the Bible, your faith, and love. Go tell people about Jesus. That's all ministry really is. The other part is laying your life down for them and making the sacrifices that obedience requires.

"Being filled with the Fruit of Righteousness, which are led by Jesus Christ, unto the Glory and Praise of God."

~ Philippians 1:11

The fruit of the Holy Spirit is righteous. The Holy Spirit enables us to follow closely behind Jesus. When we follow Jesus, we bring glory and praise to God. Hallelujah! Hallelujah! Hallelujah!

In order to close this chapter, the last scripture reference will be out of the last book of the Bible. I hope and pray you have enjoyed this

74

chapter so far as much as I have. I have faith you will hear the Word, believe the Word, and live FOR the Word so that you may bear proper fruit to benefit the Kingdom of God at large.

"In the midst of the street of it, and on either side of the river, was there the Tree of Life, which bear twelve manner of fruits, and yielded her fruit every month: and the leaves of the tree were for the *healing* of the nations."

~ Revelation 22:2

What this refers to, is the healing that must be provided for those who are not saved in the time of New Jerusalem and Heaven. Those of us who are saved will be living in glorious bodies in New Jerusalem (Heaven), while others will be on the outer skirts of Heaven needing this **healing** so that they don't get sick. Heaven provides healing. Good fruit provides healing. "A calm answer turns away wrath." Calmness is like gentleness, which is a fruit of the Holy Spirit.

Good fruit serves as a preservative for the souls of man. Good fruit is of God, so make Jesus Christ the center of your faith and bear good fruit for His glory! Amen?

"THERE CANNOT BE A MIXTURE OF BOTH GOOD AND EVIL. YOU EITHER CHOOSE JESUS AND LEARN ENOUGH ABOUT WHO HE IS SO THAT YOU MAY PRODUCE HIS KIND OF FRUIT. OR, YOU CHOOSE LIVING FOR THE WORLD AND IT'S CORRUPTION; PRODUCING BAD FRUIT."

~TY FORD

CHAPTER 6:
Prayer

"Prayer" is the most powerful weapon mankind may use. It is a spiritual weapon. A physical weapon such as a "gun" may only destroy and protect within a limited measure of reach. But, "prayer" is such a mighty weapon that expands beyond a reach we can mentally grasp. We are capable of praying for loved ones so they may be healed.

The Spirit of God does not have any boundaries. The power of prayer out stretches the confinement of the natural. Therefore, we may pray for healing and salvation for people that live many miles away. We are capable of praying joy and peace into our own lives, as well as the lives of others. We are capable of praying for financial troubles to be resolved. We are capable of praying food into our kitchen. We are capable of praying for things to happen within moments to give us a purpose for living to see tomorrow. I dare to say there is not and never will be any weapon half as powerful as "prayer." I, myself pray for God's Spirit to lead me when I teach, preach, or even write this book!

Praying men and women are the most powerful people our world beholds. What have you prayed for recently? Have you prayed with specifics?... Or, have you prayed a prayer so broad that it withholds the truth from God of what it is exactly that you want or need? Do you pray with boldness? Do you know how to pray in such a way that guarantees answers? Bear with me here as I allow the Holy Spirit to write this chapter for me.

"I can do all things through Christ who strengthens me."

~ Philippians 4:13

What am I strengthened with? "Might!" "Might" is the ability to do all things! Here we go! James 4:2 straight up tells us that, "...we have not because we ask not."

"You ask and do not receive, because you ask wrongly, to spend it on your passions."

~ James 4:3

If we never ask, we never have a chance to receive. If we ask God to meet our evil desires and not our "needs," He will not answer our prayers because He won't answer prayers that aren't within His Will. If you ask God to bring a woman into your life that is sexy and one who makes all your friends think more highly of you, God will laugh in your face! Why? Because the motives aren't pure. However, if you ask God to bring you a woman who is godly and is a servant of His, He will "show up" and "show out!" The Lord answers prayers His way and within the realm of His timing. God wants to bless us! That is why He wrote the Bible like He did. He wants us to trust in Him to meet our needs as He hears our prayer supplications. He wants us to pray with the right motives. Life is a test and guess what? It's open book. So, read! Let's say you're in college and you like to party so you ask God for a great Saturday night... You will be surprised as to how that night works out for you! You may have had something totally different in your mind when you asked that. But, God had in His mind His will to protect you, keep you safe, and show you His love.

The safest place for the brain is within the skull. The safest place for us humans to live is anywhere on earth as long as we are in the will of God. Whenever you are tempted, there is a need that is proceeding to be met. Pray that God will meet your needs His way. Tell God what it is that you need. If you are unsure, just tell Him to meet that need His own special way. Praying for God's will to be done is the most powerful prayer I honestly know of! It exemplifies "faith," "wisdom," and "trust." Jesus was in the middle of praying as He closed in on His journey to the crucifixion and He prayed:

"My Father, if this cannot pass unless I drink it, your will be done."

~Matthew 26:42

The statement Christ made to The Father represented total acquiescence of God's will. In other words, there was "no protest." God's plan for our lives are much better than anything we can dream up ourselves!

"My thoughts are completely different from yours says The Lord. And, my ways are far beyond anything you could imagine. For just as the heavens are higher than the earth, so are my ways higher than your ways, and thoughts higher than your thoughts."

~ Isaiah 55:8-9

"For I know the plans I have for you, declares The Lord, plans for welfare and not for evil, to give you a future and a hope."

~ Jeremiah 29:11

You see, God is so sovereign that His ways and thoughts truly are far beyond what we can imagine. His plans for us are better than what we could ever possibly fathom. My plans were to never be a "preacher," or an "author," or a "Sunday school teacher," or a "minister." But, God's plan has been that ever since before I was ever born. My mom always told me God had a big purpose for my life. I hung on to that for quite some time and many times doubted it, but I dare to say it kept me alive in hard times. Doing what all I do now gives me a rush so bad that it is ridiculous! I love it! I thought I loved the life I had in the "fast lane" and on "the edge." But, this life far surpasses that old lifestyle. I feel more on edge now than I ever had before!

I wage war on the enemy every single day by choosing to obey The Lord. I do not fear the enemy because I am a servant of God. I choose to place my trust in The Lord. I am a member of Christ's body. I enjoy snatching people out of the "Jaws of Hell!" When we learn and understand how it is we must pray; lives change, and many are snatched from the jaws of Hell by God's saving grace. The enemy cannot rob us without God's permission.

The story of God's servant Job relays to us how Jobs faith was strengthened, his life was restored, and he shamed the devil by his faithfulness to God when the devil robbed from him nearly everything.

I'm holding on to the love I have for Christ and will always appreciate the Cross and what all it represents. My Savior sits at the right hand of the Father and He hears my prayers. He is always listening. When we pray, He hears. Are we praying prayers in God's will? Do they match up with His Word? Are we interceding for others with the motive of love? We are capable of making withdrawals from the spiritual world with our prayers so that there is a birth that takes place in the physical world. Our prayers have the power and potential to release Heaven on to earth. We may pray for someone who has been sick with hepatitis C to be healed, and it be done in Christ Name! We literally bring Heaven to earth with our payers. We make a spiritual withdrawal from Heaven with our prayers and the fruit is in the evidence of God's answers. All of God's promises in His Word are "Yes," and "Amen!"

My friend Johnny Brown and I prayed for Jonathan Fountain to be healed of Hepatitis C. We also saw him lay down on his face and beg for God's mercy and repent. He became healed! A pastor friend of mine, named Bryan Jones, was healed by God of Hepatitis C. God heard and answered his prayers! "Boy oh Boy," it feels good to be a Child of the One True King today! Doesn't it?

The one prayer that activates the reining of the Holy Spirit in our lives is what most people refer to as the, "Sinners Prayer." This is where we admit we are a sinner and that we need mercy and grace. We believe Jesus got crucified and was raised from the dead by the glorious power of The Father. We confess that we are saved because of our faith in Jesus Christ, what He did there, and by what His Word tells us.

Paul provides us the Scriptural reference for this prayer.

"If we confess with our mouth that Jesus is Lord and believe in our hearts that God raised Him from the dead, we will be saved. For it is by believing in our hearts that we are made right with God and it is by confessing with our mouths that we are saved."

~ Romans 10:9,10

Once we pray this prayer with true intentions of being committed to Christ, we literally become saved as one of God's children. We receive a new identity. We immediately receive a new Spirit, which is God's Spirit, and is formerly known as the "Holy Spirit," which is as "holy," blameless," and "perfect" as Christ Himself. When we are saved and have the Holy Spirit at work in our lives, our prayers take on a whole new level of impact.

"A persons prayers who ignore the commands of The Lord are despised."

~ Proverbs 28:9

Before we are saved, we reject Christ and His commands. We may have prayed. But, our prayers before accepting Christ didn't have the same power as the prayers of a righteous man. Look at scripture in the book of James where it points out the power in the prayers of the righteous.

"Therefore, confess your sins to one another, and pray for one another so that you may be healed. The effective prayer of a righteous man can accomplish much. Elijah was a man with a nature like ours, and he prayed earnestly that it would not rain, and it did not rain on the earth for three years and six months. Then he prayed again, and the sky poured rain and the earth produced its fruit."

~James 5:16 - 5:18 (NASB)

Notice, Elijah was man like us. Yet, his prayers were bold, radical, dynamic, and powerful! When we give our lives to Christ and dedicate ourselves to His service, our prayers become dynamic in their working as they accomplish much. God doesn't want us to serve Him partially. God isn't looking for the tithe of our income as much as He's looking for possession of our hearts. When we let God reign in our hearts, we give Him permission to rule over our lives. When He is ruler over our lives, He is the perfecter of our faith. As He perfects our faith, He builds and equips our prayer life. The deeper we go in our relationship with Christ, the more in tune we are with God, which strengthens our prayer life. Our prayer life is strengthened by our commitment to Christ. Our prayers become more aligned with the perfect will of God as we grow in our knowledge of Who God is. We know God better by spending time with Him, reading His Word, and praying. This strengthens our service to God. Our service to God, when strengthened, serves a vital purpose as it impacts the lives of others.

When we receive salvation by calling on The Lord's Name, we should begin living life differently. We used to be sinners entangled into the ways of the world. But, when we get saved we start walking out life much differently. When we live for Christ and renew our minds with God's Word every day, we begin to shift into a new creature more and more. We begin to transform into who God designed us to be while bearing His image as His ambassadors. We can't become who God has called us to be without the power of the Holy Spirit at work in our lives.

"And now you Gentiles have also heard the truth, the Good News that God saves you. And when you believed in Christ, he identified you as his own by giving you the Holy Spirit, whom he promised long ago."

~ Ephesians 1:13

We are sealed with the Holy Spirit once we become a believer. We are first saved by the blood of Jesus Christ through the Father's love of giving His beloved Son. Then, we are sealed with the Holy Spirit. It doesn't stop at being "sealed." It all truly begins once a man is "filled" with the Holy Spirit! The physical world is birthed by the spiritual world. For example, earth did not become earth until God spoke it into existence from the spiritual dimension. We speak our lives over into the cares of The Lord as we call on His Name. When we do this, there a spiritual withdrawal that births a physical change. Our faith then springs forth evidence and fruit all along the way. What we speak has power.

Our words are capable of influencing change. When we are identified in Christ because of the relationship we have with Him, our prayers possess power. The Holy Spirit is the Strengthener and Counselor. He strengthens us with the boldness to pray radical prayers. He counsels us to discern the prayers to pray so we are within the realm of God's will with our prayers. When we are sealed with the Holy Spirit at the time of salvation, we are then prepared for the filling that takes place. When we are filled, there's not a loss for words in our prayer life. For the Word of God says, "Out of the belly shall flow rivers of living water..."

The Holy Spirit is given to us immediately following belief, acceptance, and confession. However, we may not fully realize it until a little bit later. Eventually, we will all recognize the Holy Spirit at work in our lives. The only way we may really notice it in our lives is by allowing it to be fully active. If you can drive my Ferrari but I never let you drive then I will never know how good you drive. I don't have a Ferrari and never plan on getting one even if the money were there. But, you must realize that the Holy Spirit needs two things to impact your life in mighty ways... submission and permission. When we give the Holy Spirit permission to rein we must submit to Him. In other words, we must allow Him to take the wheel. After doing this, we must be obedient to where He steers us. The grace God gives us enables our "obedience." God's ways are higher than ours and His thoughts are higher than ours. He plans to give us a hope and a future. We must trust in Him and allow Him to guide us through life. He has blessings raining down from Heaven. We shall receive from Him an abundance of life with our cups overflowing and running over as we trust in Him and believe. Let's get saved, then submit, permit, and obey!

The Holy Spirit is our Counselor, Strengthener, Advocate, and Comforter. He teaches us how to obey by convicting us of sin and counseling us how to overcome. He teaches us how to pray the prayers that are of God's will. When we get saved, we get sealed. Once we have been sealed, we are ready to be baptized, not with water, but with the Holy Spirit.

"I baptize with water those who repent of their sins and turn to God. But someone is coming soon who is greater than I am – so much greater that I'm not worthy even to be his slave and carry his sandals. He will baptize you with the Holy Spirit and with fire."

~ Matthew 3:11

Jesus baptizes us with the Holy Spirit and fire. To "baptize" means to immerse or submerse completely. In other words, when Christ baptizes us with the Holy Spirit, we become filled with the Holy Spirit! When we are filled with the Holy Spirit, we are capable of praying without ceasing, in Spirit and in truth. The blessings of God are beyond any gift from man. I am walking around with God everywhere I go. He is in me and He is active! Do I get sick? Sometimes but I speak healing into my body! I withdraw "healing" from the Spirit man so that the physical man may be healed! Are you dying? Or, are you healing? You have healing inside your inner man so withdraw it!

Christ made all the deposits we need. When we need money out of the ATM, we have to punch a few buttons right? We have to be identified and specify how much we want. With Christ, you are

84

identified as His child and you will be granted just what you need when you ask in Jesus name.

"May we shout for joy over your salvation, and in the name of our God set up for banners! May The Lord fulfill all your petitions!"

~ Psalms 20:5

This pertains to being enthusiastically joyful because of the salvation Christ has made attainable in His name. Yes, The Lord "fulfills" what we "sign" for. In other words, He meets our needs that we ask for in His Name. He answers the prayers of those who are identified with Him. Glory be to God!

Have you ever begged somebody for something? Or, do you have nasty dog that begs at the dinner table? Begging is such a turn off isn't it! When somebody begs me for something, it's like they have already been defeated for receiving anything from me. It is like they don't believe I am going to ever give them anything! God does not want to be begged by you neither. So, stop begging and start "asking with belief that you have already received!" Hallelujah! When you ask God for something, you will be better off by thanking Him already as if you've already received from Him what it is you ask for. Say, "Thank you Lord for giving me the mighty strength to get through this day topped off with that joy and peace I love so much!" Say it while you're cranky! You'll be alright! You may be cranky when you say it but brother by the time you get to work that withdrawal you made in front of your bathroom mirror has taken effect just in time for your work to be done! We can't alter the truth to match our feelings. It's better to give God praise when we feel crazy than to dilute the power of God's truth. When we speak God's Word over our lives there's a withdrawal that takes place along with a deposit.

When we pray for greater faith, we are actually withdrawing faith from Christ and depositing it into our spiritual life. Since this is a fallen world, were not always going to feel good. Praying won't always necessarily heal us and make us feels better neither. But, when we live from God's truth we are empowered by something so much greater than our mortal feelings. We are not bound by the flesh. But, empowered by the grace of God!

Give God the glory and thanks every time you receive! Sometimes, you will receive things you never even asked for but God knew you needed. God is a "sovereign" God. He is our Jehovah! He is our Jehovah Jireh also known as "The Lord who provides!" He is also our Jehovah Ropheka also known as "The Lord who heals!" I have joy in the name of Christ Jesus! I have peace I can't even explain! I have tenacity that won't allow me to ever relent in His mighty name! You must have the boldness to "ask as if you have already received!"

"Therefore I tell you, whatever you ask in prayer, believe that you have received it, and it will be yours."

~ Mark 11:24

Just make sure you believe and not doubt, because he who doubts is like a wave of the sea, blown and tossed by the wind (James 1:5,6 reference).

Do you ever doubt your boss will pay you what he owes you? Of course not! Well, some of you maybe a little "iffy" at times but if you never got paid what's been agreed you would not be there any longer. God has agreed with us in His Word what He has for us. We just have to get active with the Holy Ghost! We have to get active in prayer! We have to be obedient! We need to get caught up with our repentance! We are called to be good stewards that rightly divide the word of truth (2 Timothy 2:15 reference).

Don't ever doubt that God will not do His part! Just make sure you do yours! Receive the outpouring of the Heavens upon your life!

In the Old Testament times, men had to sacrifice animals for the omission of sins. Now, Christ has been sacrificed, which holds eternal value, meaning we no longer have to sacrifice any animals. Proverbs is of course the Old Testament and it words this truth in this manner.

"The sacrifice of the wicked is an abomination to The Lord: but the prayer of the upright is His delight."

~Proverbs 15:8

"The prayers of a person who ignores the law are despised."

~ Proverbs 28:9

If we are not willing to give our lives to Christ He really isn't willing to do anything else for us other than send messengers our way to lead us to Him. He will spare us because He has reserved us for a purpose. His goodness is what brings a man into repentance. He has already gotten crucified for us, written an instruction manual for us, and even proven to us there is eternal life. If we are unwilling to accept His salvation, what all else could we possibly expect Him to do for us?

But, once we accept His salvation we are His heirs and we have access to all that He owns, which is everything! He honors the prayers of the righteous! The righteous are those who honor Him by accepting what He has done for us at the Cross. Prayer and digesting of the Word is not something that can be done periodically and hold large impact.

"Faith comes by hearing the Word of God."

~ Romans 10:17

We must feed our faith in order to be maximized into who God has designed us to be! There is much impact in even a single prayer and a single Bible verse, but they must both be done consistently. Reading the Word of God empowers our prayer life because it strengthens our faith. When we pray, we want to do it with faith! After a while, Bible verses and prayers will be going through your mind all the time. At this point, you can afford to miss a daily reading or two because all day you were recycling what you have already read. However, there needs to be a strict routine for a year or two to lay a firm foundation of knowledge, devotion, and time to strengthen your prayer life with faith. In Mark 4, there is a sower of seed who sowed seed and some fell along the path, some fell on rocky ground, some fell among thorns, and some fell into good soil.

The 1st seed on the path got eaten by the birds.

The 2nd seed on the rocky ground sprouted up but had no depths of soil so the sun scorched it and caused it to wither away.

The 3rd seed fell among thorns and the thorns choked it out once it began to grow.

The 4th seed that fell into good soil produced some thirtyfold, some sixtyfold, and some hundredfold.

Don't allow yourself to be like any seed other than the 4th one. The ways of the world will eat you up because of the poison it possesses. People who don't read and pray daily are like the seed along rocky ground that wither away. If you hear the Word but choose to reject it then it is as if the birds robbed you of your seed immediately. But if you cultivate your mind and open your heart enough to devote to daily devotionals and prayer, you will soon produce anywhere from thirtyfold to hundredfold and sweet it will be!

"But we will give ourselves continually to prayer, and to the Ministry of the Word."

~ Acts 6:4

Praying is more important than preaching! Furthermore, praying comes first. One must have a great prayer life in order to even be used influentially as a preacher. One's prayer life is ultimately strengthened by the relationship they have with Jesus Christ.

Salvation is free, but the anointing will cost you everything! This chapter has placed a large emphasis on the Holy Spirit because He plays a huge role in our prayer life. He is our Counselor, Strengthener, Advocate, Comforter, and Standby. When we sow into our spiritual life by continuous interaction with the Holy Spirit, we reap the advantages of the relationship as He's always there ready and on "standby." When we spend time with God consistently, we won't have trouble learning how to pray. We won't miss out on understanding the power of prayer neither. The relationship has benefits!

So, get in the Word and pray with the knowledge the Word offers to you. Get in God's will and surrender to it. Pray for others. Pray for all nations. Pray for peace. Pray for the sick. Pray for schools. Pray for authority. Pray for Christians and pray for the lost. Lastly, pray for yourself. Amen.

Thank you for bearing with me as I prayed my way through this chapter!

"INTEGRITY IS A MILESTONE TO REACH, BUT IS ATTAINABLE THROUGH THE GRACE OF GOD AND TEACHINGS OF CHRIST. "

~ TY FORD

CHAPTER 7:
Respect

There are moments in all of our lives where we "demand" respect. There are just as many moments that we are unwilling to "give" respect. How can we possibly demand respect that we are unwilling to give. Demanding respect and refusing to give respect to those in honor are both similar in the way that they are our flesh acting out. In other words, these are our "natural inclinations." How can we possibly give the kind of respect that we wish to receive? How do we earn it and how do we give it? Let's see what Scripture has to say about "respect" so that we can move right on along in life with a level of respect that is approved by God.

Malachi 1:6-14 tells us how angry The Lord may get when we don't do as we should. It refers here to sacrifices from people of animals who are "crippled" and "blind." We are to give the best of our assets to The Lord. We are to use our talents for The Lord first and tithe before we spend.

"A son honors his father, and a servant his master. If then I am a father, where is my honor? And if I am a master, where is my fear? says the Lord of hosts to you, O priests, who despise my name. But you say, 'How have we despised your name?' By offering polluted food upon my altar. But you say, 'How have we polluted you?' By saying that the Lord's table may be despised. When you offer blind animals in sacrifice, is that not evil? And when you offer those that are lame or sick, is that not evil? Present that to your governor; will he accept you or show you favor? says the Lord of hosts. And now entreat the favor of God, that he may be gracious to us.

With such a gift from your hand, will he show favor to any of you? says the Lord of hosts. Oh that there were one among you who would shut the doors, that you might not kindle fire on my altar in

vain! I have no pleasure in you, says the Lord of hosts, and I will not accept an offering from your hand. For from the rising of the sun to its setting my name will be great among the nations, and in every place incense will be offered to my name, and a pure offering.

For my name will be great among the nations, says the Lord of hosts. But you profane it when you say that the Lord's table is polluted, and its fruit, that is, its food may be despised. But you say, 'What a weariness this is,' and you snort at it, says the Lord of hosts. You bring what has been taken by violence or is lame or sick, and this you bring as your offering! Shall I accept that from your hand? says the Lord. Cursed be the cheat who has a male in his flock, and vows it, and yet sacrifices to the Lord what is blemished. For I am a great King, says the Lord of hosts, and my name will be feared among the nations."

~ Malachi 1:6-14

If The Lord gives us something, how can we possibly not give the best of what He gave us back to Him. If everything we receive is from The Lord, then how can we possibly be so greedy that we are unwilling to give Him what He is more than worthy of? This is a sure sign of "disrespect!" This shows Him no gratitude and no acceptable service. If we are to serve The Lord we ought to do our best!

God points out to us how offering our worst would get us killed with the government. So, how should we expect God to continually bless us if we won't show Him any respect? This is all inclusive to "disobedience" which God never blesses. He blesses our obedience and disciplines us for our disobedience. 2 Corinthians 8:8 says, "we give to The Lord to prove the sincerity of our love" (paraphrased).

The Priests are those held responsible in this situation because they should have known better than to allow contaminated sacrifices to be offered up to The Lord. Disrespect is direct disobedience to God.

In Malachi, we learned what it is to be disrespectful to The Lord directly. In Titus, we will learn here what it is to earn respect and with what qualities qualify for it. Chapter 2, verse 2 says, "Teach the older men to exercise self-control, to be worthy of respect, and to live wisely. They must have strong faith and be filled with love and patience." Self-control and patience are both part of the Fruit of the Spirit. They must both be exercised together as one in order to earn the kind of respect that brings unity to a church or ministry. If I lose my temper when someone gets out of line at Fourth Day Transition House, I will not be exercising self-control. To live wisely and be even tempered develops character that is "worthy of respect." I must be patient with others and compassionate for their behavior. Behavioral issues are only temporary for most that walk into the doors at Fourth Day Ministries. Why?

Because as the Holy Spirit works on these men, their old behaviors become "dead and gone." They are "gone and passed away." Behold, "all things become new!" 2 Corinthians 5:17 tells us that when we become in Christ the old person passes away while the new man shows itself. It takes "love" in order for anyone to earn respect in any ministry, church, or even work environment of any kind. For us to respect our bosses we must love them. It's hard for the non-believer or even the young Christian to love their boss or authority figure if they don't experience any sign of love by them first. Scripture tells us, "We love Him because He loved us first." Therefore, leaders in the church are called to a standard that demonstrates love.

We have learned about disrespecting God directly in Malachi. We have learned how to live in such a way that earns respect in Titus. Now, we will venture off to Ephesians 5:33 where it discusses the relationship between a husband and wife:

"So again I say, each man must love his wife as he loves himself, and the wife must respect her husband."

~ Ephesians 5:33

The whole divine idea of marriage is "unity" or "becoming as one." That is why the husband must love his wife as he does himself because in terms of the divine idea, both are unified. The husband and wife must both recognize that Christ is their Savior and not the wife nor the husband! The wife must look to Christ just like the husband must look at Christ. It would only be unfair to look at one another for the solution to everyday problems. Love does not conquer all in relationships. JESUS does!

The wife is one bottom leg of the triangle while the husband is the other and Christ is the center top point of the entire triangle. Most marriages today fail because of their improper understanding of this concept. Christ must be at the center. It is disrespectful for either spouse to depend on one another the way they should depend on Christ alone. It is senseless for a married couple to look to one another the way they are called to look to Christ. No human is qualified to be another humans "Savior." The husband is called to love his wife like Christ loves the church. This means becoming a professional forgiver constantly filled with compassion. The wife is called to respect her husband. This means submitting to her husband and honoring him.

"In the same way, you wives must accept the authority of your husbands. Then, even if some refuse to obey the Good News, your godly lives will speak to them without any words. They will be won over by observing your pure and reverent lives."

~1 Peter 3:1-2

To respect someone is to honor them in such a way that it resembles Christ like behavior. For example, when the husband is making decisions that the wife knows are not best, but she honors him anyway. The husband could be won over to Christ by the wife's faithfulness, submission, and respect. Then, because of respect that was given to him, he could become the spiritual leader he is called to be through Christ.

So, now we have covered respectfulness to God directly, being qualified for respect, and the right measure of respect in a marriage. The next area to cover is leadership in a church. A leader in a church must first be qualified before he can even be respected. If a church allowed anyone to step in for leadership there would be a whole lot of disrespect going on.

"He must manage his own family well, with children who respect and obey him. For if a man cannot manage his own household, how can he take care of God's church?"

~1 Timothy 3:4,5

One must be respected already before he can begin to qualify as a respected leader in a church. I have a family of my own, but also treat those who I deal with in ministry like they are my family. In all reality, through Christ we are family. While working at Mercy House Ministries, my fellow brothers made up the "Timothy's" and "Paul's" in my life. Some of them I ministered to while others ministered to me. I had to take on the role as a leader at Mercy House before I could be qualified as a leader for my church body. Then I had to do both before being entrusted with Fourth Day Ministries.

This reminds me of Matthew 25 where Jesus talks about the talents or gifts that we must be entrusted with well before we receive anymore. If we can't invest what we are given first, how can we invest an increase wisely?

I have moved several times since I first graduated the Teen Challenge associated program, Mercy House Ministries. Each time I have moved has been a step up. Before every move I became more responsible by cleaning up and taking care of what I had been given. I am still working my way up to my own house. Right now I have an RV that is in my mind very nice, but it has some electrical issues that I am in the middle of figuring out how to fix. Nonetheless, I am happy because this is a gift from God and I will take care of it well because

His Word tells me that a house will soon be a reality of mine that I will be living in. Become a great leader by handling each responsibility you are entrusted with well. Grow in what you've been entrusted with.

Develop leadership skills and grow in stewardship. (I testify when I say that 2 years after originally writing this chapter I will live in a beautiful house with a beautiful family that makes it a wonderful home). As 2 years have passed since first writing this book, I became married; I married into being a father to two; Shortly after marriage we had a newborn son to make it the third. Then we bought a home in Mobile, AL. Now we are getting ready to move into an even bigger home in Meridian, MS. God is good! Our tongue determines the course of our life. I spoke I would live in a home with my own family within 2 years and it came to pass right at 2 years later. What are you speaking over your life? God is faithful! He has all the sources. To us they are just resources. He has called us to be good stewards of all that He blesses us with.

Some men may desire to become a deacon rather than a teacher or preacher because it does not require as much responsibility. Maybe few people feel like that by being a deacon there are activities they partake in they won't have to give up because they are only a deacon and not a minister.

"In the same way, deacons must be people who are respected and have integrity. They must not be heavy drinkers and must not be greedy for money."

~1 Timothy 3:8

If you bar-tend at a club where you take shots behind the scenes on every hour this probably isn't the job for you. If you work for a company that rips off its clients and lacks integrity, you probably aren't necessarily qualified neither.

Not that either of these jobs are bad, but what's the reason for working the job? Jesus could have turned a stone into a loaf of bread and it not be bad. But, not for the devil when he presents the idea to Him as a temptation.

There may be nothing wrong with either of these jobs. But, why work there? What is your reasoning behind it? I can understand if you are non-drinker that serves alcohol to ensure it is served responsibly while screening those who say they can drive home. Maybe you bartend to ensure safety within the night life. That would be acceptable. But, are you bar-tending to find those of the opposite sex while they are vulnerable so you can take them home? Are you bartending so you can drink for free while on the job? Are you bar-tending so you can steal liquor so you save your habitual cost? Why and for what reason do you do what you do? As far as the company that lacks integrity goes, are you working the job because it pays well or are you working inside such an environment to ensure grace and integrity? Integrity speaks volumes!

Integrity is a milestone to reach, but is attainable through the grace of God and teachings of Christ. Evaluate your life at this very moment and see what changes you may need to make. There may not be any changes you believe you need to make and that could be either good or bad. Either way, it is up to you to better yourself. When you want to better yourself, Jesus Christ is the answer! His character incorporated into your life equals "success" and growth" and "maturity."

As far as being a wife goes or as far as teaching your wife how to be in order to avoid public controversy, **1 Timothy 3:11** says, **"In the same way, their wives must be respected and must not speak evil of others. They must exercise self-control and be faithful in everything they do."** So if you have a "gossiping" wife, you better let her know that she can't do that. If she already does that, she needs to stop. Either way, let your wife know what God's Word says about this because there is a reason God included it in His Word. Strife stems from gossip. Gossip grows into strife. And, strife breeds hate, which is evil.

"Again I say, don't get involved in foolish ignorant arguments that only start fights. The Lord's servants must not quarrel but must be kind to everyone and be patient with difficult people."

~2 Timothy 2:23,24

Gossip leads to arguments and arguments lead to fights. Fights cause division. In other words, stay away from gossip for respect of The Lord and the church. Self-control is the department out of the Fruit of the Spirit that must be exercised in order to avoid such division among the church. Love for Christ must be the motivating factor to strive towards a level of self-control that prevents gossip, which prevents arguments, which prevents strife, which prevents fights, which prevents division among the church body.

The last Scripture we will cover in this chapter concerning respect is 1 Peter 2:17.

"Show respect for everyone. Love your Christian brothers and sisters. Fear God. Show respect for the King."

~1 Peter 2:17

The only way to show respect for the King is by having an approved level of respect for all men and women. He who honors The Lord will not dishonor any man.

How many times have you not given someone in authority who is in your life the proper level of respect? We have all fell short from time to time.

"We have all sinned and fallen short of God's glory, being justified as a gift by God's grace through the redemption which is in Christ Jesus."

~ Romans 3:23, 24

Thank God for His grace. If you have not done as well as you wish you had in respecting God or people in your life.... Today is the day to rise up to the challenge! Today is an opportunity for you to repent and change your mind in a way that breeds obedience. Now, you may be empowered by "unmerited favor," "tender, loving kindness," "mercy," and "grace."

Have you been saved? If not, right now is the very moment you may allow Christ to take the reins of your life since you have been discontent with the way you have been living.

Admit you are a sinner.

Believe Christ is Lord and Savior. Understand He died one moment for you alone. One moment He thought only of you. For one moment, you were all that went through His mind while He died on the Cross. It took many moments and every moment equaled one person. He died for us all but for one moment you were all that was on His mind and He was so faithful to do it.

Confess your righteousness in Jesus Christ. Yes. Because you are now a believer, you are righteous through Jesus Christ. In Jesus Christ name, YOU are RIGHTEOUS! Righteous through your faith in Him. Can I get a HALLELUJAH!? Better yet, can HE get a HALLELUJAH!? Say, "Thank You Jesus!" You have now been instantly sealed by the Holy Spirit. Mercy, tender loving kindness, grace, and unmerited favor are the components by which you have been sealed with.

You have now a Helper, Counselor that is as perfect, blameless, and faultless as Jesus Christ Himself! Journey on through the rest of your week carrying your own cross to follow Jesus while knowing that you have been sealed by Grace!

"IF THE LORD GIVES US SOMETHING HOW CAN WE POSSIBLY NOT GIVE THE BEST OF WHAT HE GAVE US BACK TO HIM."

~TY FORD

CHAPTER 8:
Love

"What's love got to do with it?" The answer to that question is, "EVERYTHING!"

Love is God and God is love. Love is what endures forever. Love makes the world go round. Love is what connects people. Love is what connects people to their passion. Love is what drives people towards the careers they choose. Love is what causes people to give. Love is what allows people to receive. Love is everywhere all of the time, but how?!

The answer is, "GOD!" God is everywhere all the time because He is omnipresent. Everywhere God is, love is there as well. We can be mad at times but at the flip of a switch we can turn it into love, compassion, and forgiveness. This is because love is surrounding us and in us.

"Christ is all that matters and He lives in all of us."

~ Colossians 3:11

Jesus died on the Cross just for you for one moment.

For one moment, you were all He had on His mind! It took many moments in that day for Him to actually die. I dare to say that for just one of those moments He died for you and for you alone!

God is a personal God and He desires a personal and intimate relationship with you. He died for you to reconcile you to Himself. We should all be dead by justice but because of love and grace we are all still here today. God has a significant purpose for you in the life you are given. You are made to make a significant difference that serves a large impact for Him and His Kingdom. We are called to serve Him by serving others. John 3:16 tells us how much God loves us.

What does 1 John 3:16 say though? It tells us:

"We know what real love is because Christ gave up His life for us. And so we also ought to give up our lives for our Christian brothers and sisters."

~1 John 3:16

God served us by giving up His life for us so that we may be inspired to lay our lives down for others. God wants us to take up our cross and follow Him. When we do this we become so over-showered with blessings that it changes our lives and changes who we are. It enhances our lives by the billions! So what does love have to do with it? Or, what does God have to do with love? Is love God? Is God love? Do you have God in your heart without even realizing it? If there is any love in you at all then yes you do! 1 Corinthians 13 tells us all about love. We would not have a chance of knowing love if there were not a God. We would not have a power higher than us if there were not a LIVING GOD who we know as Jesus Christ.

The reliability and credibility of the Gospels are the most reliable and credible piece of history there has ever been. If the Gospels don't count in the history books then what possibly could? I recommend anyone and everyone to check out Lee Strobel's, *Case For Christ*. This book clarifies the history of the Gospels and their reliability. The Jewish people recorded history better than anyone. They did not exaggerate or change the information to appease the people. They passed on history by reciting it religiously and faithfully.

They were perfectionists! Lee Strobel was an atheist set out to prove there wasn't a God in his book, *Case For A Creator*. He tried to also prove the Gospels were not correct about the death, burial, and resurrection of Christ. In both books, Strobel found his own theories to be false. He realized Jesus did die, was buried, and became resurrected! He also found that the chances of there not being a God were so astronomical it was out of this world. Science actually therefore supports theology in the sense of Jesus Christ being the LIVING GOD. If God were dead how would there still be love?

The world has taken some drastic turns for the worse. But, in the midst of these storms in the world, God has moved in people and has caused them to do some extraordinary things in helping people who are suffering. Helping the poor. Helping the storm victims.

Helping cancer patients for free, like St. Jude. There may be a lot of evil and hate in the world today but if you are in the Kingdom you experience the work of God in many areas. When you are in the world and have a worldly point of view you see the bad and tend to focus on it all. However, when you are in the Kingdom of God you are connected and plugged into the greatness of God. You hear about and see much more love than you ever knew there was in such a world. I used to be in the world, had a worldly mindset, and went hard for the world by the drugs I sold and evil sins I committed. Now, I am a devout and radical Christian plugged into a lot of greatness that is going on today.

I experience God's love by the people I encounter. I witness some extraordinary things by the churches, ministries, and organizations I am involved with! God is good and He is good all the time. Love is here and love is there. Love is everywhere. Wherever you are and no matter what you are going through, love encompasses you while it is also inside of you. If Colossians 3:11 tells us that Christ is in all of us and He is all that matters, then what exactly is that saying? Well, Christ symbolically represents love in itself. Dying for you and me just to have a relationship with us is love in an extreme. If that same Spirit that raised Him from the dead lives in us then we are filled with love! By "filled," I mean FILLED! He is all that matters. Love is all that matters. Love makes the biggest difference on this planet! What does love have to do with it!? And, what does God have to do with love!? Everything! By "everything," I mean EVERYTHING!

"Love is patient and kind. Love is not jealous or boastful or proud or rude. Love does not demand its own way. Love is not irritable and it keeps no record of when it has been wronged. It is never glad about injustice but rejoices whenever the truth wins out. Love never gives up. never loses faith, is always hopeful, and endures through every circumstance."

~ 1 Corinthians 13:4-7

Love is SO AWESOME! How much of a difference can we all make in each other's lives with this type of love? There are 3 different kinds of love.

There is "Eros" love, which is erotic or sexual love.

There is "Philein" love, which is brotherly kindness.

There is also "Agape" love, which is Godly love.

This love mentioned here in 1 Corinthians is true agape or "godly" love. It is the best kind of love. While being patient and kind we are very understanding and compassionate for others. It causes us to be considerate of others rather than selfish. By not being jealous or boastful or proud or rude we are kind, humble, and effective. By not demanding our own way we are yielding to others feelings and putting ourselves last.

"But many who are first will be last, and the last first."

~Matthew 19:30

It is better to put ourselves last because it is yielding to others and putting them first. In order to put God first we must put others first.

When we hold no account of irritability we are patient and able to endure the circumstances we are in. As we do this, we exemplify a type of love that will cause people to be astonished. And, as they become astonished and wonder where this love comes from we are then able to witness to them by telling them just exactly where we get our love from and who this love is. If I hold record of being wrong I will forever hold a resentment. I will hold a grudge that the waves of Hawaii can't break down. If I keep no record of something that is said or done to make me feel inadequate or inferior, then there always lies a fresh start. Love can then be established and growth may take place.

This life as we know it on this planet is all about relationships. Relationship with the Father and relationships with people in general. While love holds an eternal value and we are filled with love, we are able to keep on trucking our way through life without ever giving up. Whether you have admitted God is love yet or not, it is what drives you through life striving and seeking to do what is right. For me, it is Jesus that propels me through life. It is grace and the Holy Spirit that empower me to do the "above and beyond."

We are no longer under subjection to the Mosaic Law such as all that was given in the Old Testament and the Book of Exodus around the 20th Chapter. The Ten Commandments were given to us to prove that we could not uphold such laws and commands. It allowed us to search for something greater like a Savior, Jesus Christ. Could you imagine living in the old times of such laws where you tried and tried and tried to uphold the laws and commands but failed miserably every single day? I can sure imagine that! I would wonder daily when this Messiah was to come and bail me out of my own iniquities. Thank God for grace. Thank God for compassion. Thank God for sovereignty. Thank God for love! Now we are not held to such standards, laws, and commands without grace that empowers us.

Jesus did not come to abolish the law, but to fulfill it! He gives us grace that empowers godly living. Now it is real simple. We are told by Jesus to love God with all our soul, mind, heart, and strength.

"I have a new commandment for you. Love one another the way I have loved you. In doing this, you will prove to the world that you are my disciples."

~ John 13:34,35

That makes it pretty simple, yet still challenging. We love God completely and love people like God loves us. God tells us that when we keep these two laws we keep from breaking any of the old ones. For example, you won't covet while operating under love. You won't commit adultery while operating under love. You won't kill someone under the influence and standard of love. You won't fall into idolatry while you're in love with God. Under grace, we are given the commandments of love, which protect us from disobeying the Ten Commandments. Our focus is love instead of a focus of "do's and don'ts." We are empowered by grace with a standard of love that keeps us from sowing into the flesh and reaping from the flesh it's corruption and consequences!

We are now under the law of grace and not our old sinful nature.

"Since we have been united with Him in His death, we will also be raised as He was. Our old sinful selves were crucified with Christ so that sin might lose its power in our lives. We are no longer slaves to sin. For when we died with Christ we were set free from the power of sin. And since we died with Christ, we know we will also share His new life."

~ Romans 6:5-8

We are no longer trespassers because we have been pardoned. If you have a friend in prison or jail but has been pardoned, they will be let out as a free citizen without any record against them. We have been released from the bondage we so long dwelled in. It is a great day to be alive when you know that you can live in peace because of the love that encompasses you and dwells within your mortal body.

God has been loving us since the very beginning of time. After the sins of Adam and Eve we should have all never been born. But, because of His love, compassion, and desire to have a relationship with us He has been chasing us down ever since the beginning of time. He constantly knocks on the door to our hearts.

"Look! Here I stand at the door and knock. If you hear me calling and open the door, I will come in and we will share a meal as friends."

~ Revelation 3:20

He wants to be our friend! He is a best friend to any man or woman that lets Him in their heart!

"There are friends who destroy each other but a real friend sticks closer than a brother."

~ Proverbs 18:24

Jesus is a "real friend that sticks closer than a brother." Brothers fight; but Jesus will stick to you closer than a brother with the mission of completing you and making you whole. Every moment of every day Jesus is right there with us as we marinate in His presence.

"Remember, O Lord, your unfailing love and compassion, which you have shown from long ages past."

~ Psalm 25:6

David here reminds God of the love He has continuously and constantly shown to us. God is patient. Patience may be defined as being "consistently constant."

Think of all the sin you have lived in and how good God has been to you even in the midst of all your worst days. The goodness of God is what brings us into repentance. God has allowed us to be rained down on with His mercy so that one day He can have the relationship with us He desires. Once we surrender to Him and bond with Him in such a relationship, we then find a whole other dimension of life on this planet that we never knew even existed!

"Your unfailing love to me is better to me than life itself; how I praise you!"

~ Psalm 25:6

How can we possibly praise God? Showing our love to others is a great way to use the love God has entrusted us with and put it to good use.

John 13:34, 35 tells us this as we have gone over previously. When I receive love I have love to offer. When I offer love, I receive more. The more I receive, the more I have to offer.

Matthew 25 talks about 3 men given talents. 1 man received 5, another 2, and another 1. The 2 men that received 5 and 2 invested theirs wisely to accumulate interest. The man who received 1 buried the 1 talent in the dirt. Who do you think the Master rewarded and who do you think he didn't? He rewarded the first two men who accumulated interest by giving them more and he cut off the man who was unwise and buried the talent into the dirt.

The same goes for us with love. We sow what we reap so we may reap more. The more we reap the more we sow and vice versa.

"Do not be deceived for God is not mocked: for whatsoever a man sows, that he shall also reap."

~ Galatians 6:7

If you sow love, you reap love. If you reap grace you better sow some because you will surely need more sooner than you think!

Love has a lot to do with everything around you and inside you. Remember that God is love and love is God. God is good and God is good all the time. You can't love anyone without God's hand involved. You may be an atheist but if you love your spouse, then guess what? That's God! If you are married, then guess what? You got married because of your knowledge of what marriage consists of. Where do we learn about marriage? The Bible. If you love anyone then you have God inside you. It's just a matter of accepting God to really release all that He has to offer. We must accept Him as Lord over our lives and the Redeemer of our souls. We may have love in us, but we must furthermore give Christ Lordship over our lives and we will discover even more. The blessings of God are always present in your life but it is when you accept Christ that they are profound! When you obey the teachings of Christ, His blessings manifest in your life. In doing so, others are blessed because of your obedience. Faith the size of a mustard seed starts off real small, but in due season it grows into a tree that provides nests for the birds. Your faith can grow into a shelter for others. Your faith can develop for others what they can't develop for themselves. Your faith can empower a love for hurting people in hopes that they will grow strong in their faith and love as well.

The Kingdom of God is all about the multiplication of disciples. Enjoy your day, your week, and your life because love is in the air and it is everywhere! Seek and you shall find. Glory to God!

"LOVE HAS A LOT TO DO WITH EVERYTHING AROUND YOU AND INSIDE YOU. REMEMBER THAT GOD IS LOVE AND LOVE IS GOD. GOD IS GOOD AND GOD IS GOOD ALL THE TIME. YOU CAN'T LOVE ANYONE WITHOUT GOD'S HAND INVOLVED."

~ TY FORD

CHAPTER 9:
Salvation

My Salvation has nothing to do with what I have done but everything to do with what He has done!

Sure, I accepted the free gift of eternal life but I have not earned it. I cannot earn it. Jesus earned it for everybody. For those of us who believe in Him, accept Him as our Lord, and choose to take up our cross and follow Him; receive a gift beyond comprehension.

I throw you a telephone and you use it. Congratulations, you have used something I earned for you. I earned the money to buy the telephone and gave it to you. Now, you may use it to call whoever you choose to whether it be national or international because that's how good I am to you. It is nice to be able to make some calls around the world but isn't it much nicer to know that the whole world has been called?

"For many are called but few are chosen."

~ Matthew 22:14

Speaking of telephones, Jesus is calling everybody right now and has been since the beginning of time.

"In the beginning the Word already existed. He was with God, and He was God. He was in the beginning with God. He created everything there is. Nothing exists that He didn't make."

~John 1:1-3

This is Jesus we are talking about here! He has been at work since before the earth ever came to know Him. When Moses led the

Israelites on their journey through the wilderness do you think that the Father was alone in His work? No. Of course not.

"Do you not believe that I am in the Father and the Father is in me? The words that I say to you I do not speak on my own authority, but the Father who dwells in me does His works. Believe me that I am in the Father and the Father is in me, or else believe on account of the works themselves."

~ John 14:10,11

Jesus is the way, the truth, and the life. Therefore, Him being truth we must believe this as the truth. Jesus and the Father are connected just like the Holy Spirit is with us. The Father has pre-ordained Jesus and His death on the Cross. This is so we may have eternal life and the devil may be overtaken. Jesus rose from the dead and revealed Himself to somewhere around 500 people. He left because by Him leaving, the Holy Spirit may enter into our lives as the wonderful counselor He is. The supernatural is still here. Lame men still walk. Deaf men still hear. And, blind men do see. Dead men have been raised from the dead not only in Acts but since then as well.

The mid 1900's there was a man named Smith Wigglesworth, and there are documentations recorded of him raising people from the dead not on his own authority, but in Jesus Christ name. I recommend for you to read about him. People wonder where God is today because they don't want to get in line with Him and perform the supernatural. People want to hear about God but many fail to read His Word. People want their lives to be simple and smooth but not many want to pray and study the character of Jesus Christ nor discover the supernatural power of the Holy Ghost.

"What good is it, my brothers, if someone says he has faith but does not have works? Can that faith save him?"

~James 2:14

Faith apart from works is dead just like works without faith is dead. I can't go to Heaven by being a good person. Why?

Because no matter how good I may be in comparison to the evil world, I still have sinful nature that resides within me. Without accepting Christ that sinful nature is what dwells within my mortal body, but upon acceptance of Christ I was washed in the blood, redeemed, and received the Spirit of Christ, also referred to as the Holy Spirit. Now, I have redemption.

I was a drug addict hooked on cocaine and heroin with dirty needles contaminating my living space, but now I have been delivered! I served the world its drugs ethically and treated the people with dignity and respect until I was dealt a bad hand. I was a good person in an evil, wicked world. When I caught a glimpse of evil I spread it down the line. In other words, if someone robbed me I robbed them back. Or, maybe I robbed someone else. I was a good person until the "junk hit the fan."

"But now O' Israel, The Lord who created you says, 'Do not be afraid, for I have ransomed you. I have called you by name and you are mine!'"

~ Isaiah 43:1

He has ransomed me, delivered me, redeemed me, and freed me all at the same time.

"There is power in the name of Jesus, to break every chain, break every chain, and break every chain!"

~Tasha Cobb

Now, the good that I do is backed by my faith in Jesus Christ. The bad I do is sin that the Holy Spirit inside me refuses to participate in. After it's said and done, He convicts me for it so that I may learn, grow, and repent. I confess my righteousness in Christ Jesus.

"For we all have sinned and fall short of the glory of God, being justified as a gift by His grace through the redemption which is found in Christ Jesus."

~Romans 3:23,24

I still sin. But, I no longer live in it. I used to live under the law of sinful nature but now I live under the law of grace and its Spirit of Life. Just because I have been saved and am destined for Heaven does not mean that I am now just as holy as Christ is ALL the time. However, I'm baptized with the Holy Spirit which makes me holy and blameless in the eyes of God. Covered by the blood and baptized in the Spirit causes God to see you as faultless.

Now I'm on fire living for the Lord and I'm set out to disciple the poor and minister to the lost.

Faith has changed my works. My works before were good in my poor sighted judgement. Even if I never cussed, drank, nor smoked, and gave one thousand dollars to charity every month... those works would have still been useless without Jesus Christ as my Lord and Savior. Jesus died for you! Why won't you accept it?

Don't be so stubborn and hard-headed! He died for you!

He died for you! He shed blood for you! For one moment of that glorious day it was all for you and for you alone! You're a sinner as bad as that sounds, and as hard as that is to hear, it is the TRUTH!

You can't be holy without holiness in you! You can't go to a holy place without being holy. There are certain islands you can't get to without a watercraft just like Heaven is a place that good works won't get you to. You have to accept Christ into your heart.

"For if you confess with your mouth that Jesus is Lord and believe in your heart that God raised Him from the dead, you will be saved. For it is by believing in your heart that you are made right with God and it is by confessing with your mouth that you are saved."

~Romans 10:9,10

Nike used to have a slogan known as, "JUST DO IT!" That's my motto with salvation. Just do it! Give it a shot! Are there Christians who are stumbling blocks!? Absolutely!

Are there football players who smoke cigarettes and aren't that good? Yes. As a matter of fact, I used to smoke and do all kinds of drugs. I was good, but still, my actions did not match my identity.

There are Christians who claim their Savior but they live immorally. Guess what? Jesus loves them anyway!

"Then Peter came up and said to him, 'Lord, how often will my brother sin against me, and I forgive him? As many as seven times?' Jesus said to him, 'I do not say to you seven times, but seventy times seven."

~Matthew 18:21,22

How could you possibly keep track of 490 times to forgive someone. There are many people we must continuously forgive, and not just one. Therefore, who's counting? Just keep forgiving. We are commanded to continuously forgive others including our Christian brothers and sisters. Now then, isn't it safe to assume that Jesus also continuously forgives us for our sins, willful or not, throughout the remainder of our lives after the time we accept Him into our lives?

Of course He does, because that's just how good God is! Now, don't act to quick on that because what we do on earth these days as we know it determines our place in the Kingdom for eternity. Christians who are faithful and disciples who are active in ministry will all take on a significant place in eternity. Those who take advantage of their salvation by falling away from it and sinning willfully will be judged for it and possibly forfeit their place in God's Kingdom. A spot in God's Kingdom is received by the blood and kept by faithful endurance. So be faithful and endure until the end.

"But he who endures to the end shall be saved."

~ Matthew 24:13 (NKJV)

"Now the just shall live by faith; But if anyone draws back, My soul has no pleasure in him."

~Hebrews 10:38 (NKJV)

We must endure hardships and trials while upholding our relationship with The Lord. In marriage, both the man and the woman are called to be faithful and endure through better and worse. It is the same with our relationship to the Lord. We must remain faithful and endure the good times and the hard ones as well. God doesn't find pleasure in those who are deliberately sinning. Hebrews 10:26 tells us if we go on deliberately sinning there's no longer a sacrifice for our sins. Relationship with the Lord is serious business. It's not meant to be taken lightly. A child of God is committed to Him through the blood covenant of Jesus Christ.

Take the Gospel to places you would never go on your own will. Grab a partner and go off in "two's" like Jesus sent His disciples off to minister before. Be willing to minister to anyone, anywhere, at any time.

As disciples of Christ, we never know when an opportunity may arise for us to make a positive difference carrying the light to darkness. One night I was shopping at Best Buy when a young girl let out a "bloody murder" type cry. I didn't know what in the world was going on until I realized her brother had gotten killed. So I said a prayer for her family on my way home that night.

"Then if my people who are called by my name will humble themselves, pray, seek my face, and turn away from their wicked ways, I will hear from Heaven, will forgive their sins, and heal their land."

~2 Chronicles 7:14

God is so good that none of us can truly experience nor fathom the sovereignty of His grace. Many of us want to cast people out of Heaven for their sins and send them to Hell, but God is much bigger and better than that. Every Christian and every disciple will be disciplined for their actions by what they did do and what they didn't do. God does not send people to Hell. People unfortunately send themselves there by rejecting Jesus Christ. God helps people by doing all He can to lead them into the promise land. Christ died for us all and it doesn't stop there. He died for us and constantly longs for us.

"Look! Here I stand at the door and knock. If you hear me calling and open the door, I will come in and we will share a meal as friends."

~ Revelation 3:20

Jesus knocks on the door to our heart every moment of every single day. He does this for all of us, believers or not. He gives us all as many opportunities as possible to get it right and resort to Him with everything and in everything.

"There are friends who destroy each other, but a real friend sticks closer than a brother."

~ Proverbs 18:24

Sovereignty of Christ

This brother of ours is known as Jesus Christ. He soothes us with His grace and strengthens us with His might. He's always with us no matter how far away He feels and no matter how much He is out of our sight. He keeps our temptations from becoming too strong to stand up against. He is faithful and He always shows us a way out.

"And remember that the temptations that come into your life are no different from what others experience. And God is faithful. He will keep the temptation from becoming so strong that you can't stand up against it. When you are tempted, He will show you a way out so that you will not give in to it."

~ 1 Corinthians 10:13

Sin is easy to fall into and a grueling journey to depart from. Remember though, we now live under the law of grace and Spirit of Life.

"Remember it is a sin to know what you ought to do and then not do it."

~ James 4:17

It is a sin to do what we shouldn't do and also a sin to not do what we should do. But, by the law of grace we are the righteousness of God in Christ Jesus.

"Therefore, since we have been made right in God's sight by faith, we have peace with God because of what Jesus Christ our Lord has done for us."

~ Romans 5:1

The Father sent His Son Jesus Christ to die as a sinner, although a perfect man, so that we sinners could be reconciled to Himself and share in all His glory. We are as filthy dirty rags without Jesus. Our sins died on the Cross with Christ Jesus. What year did that happen?

Ok, now what year is it today? The sins of yours today and your sins tomorrow have all already been taken care of!

"Well then, should we keep on sinning so that God can show us more and more of His kindness and forgiveness? Of course not! Since we have died to sin, how can we continue to live in it?"

~Romans 6:1-2

We are the righteousness of God in Christ Jesus! So, don't walk around feeling condemned.

"So now there is no condemnation for those who belong to Christ Jesus."

~ Romans 8:1

You belong to Christ Jesus right? Well stop feeling condemned!

Don't allow your enemies to condemn you. Don't give the enemy any more power than he already has! Do you feel guilty because you don't have Christ? Well get Him! Everybody needs a good friend that will stick closer than a brother. Once you accept Christ you receive the free gift of eternal life.

"For the wages of sin is death but the free gift of God is eternal life through Christ Jesus our Lord."

~ Romans 6:23

Once you receive salvation you automatically and immediately receive the Holy Spirit.

"And now you also have heard the truth, the Good News that God saves you. And when you believed in Christ, He identified you as His own by giving you the Holy Spirit, whom He promised long ago."

~ Ephesians 1:13

Sovereignty of Christ

Once you believe, you receive more than you can at first handle. It takes forever to walk accordingly to all that you receive. You have received salvation and you have received a Spirit that resides inside you stronger than a lion. The same Spirit that raised Christ from the dead also lives inside you. What are you going to do with it?

Are you going to walk around indulging in sin that separates you from this Spirit where you will "sin unto death?" Or, are you going to test the waters and see just how powerful this Spirit inside you is willing to come alive and be released?

"Greater is He in you than he that lives in the world outside."

~1 John 4:4

Now, *"Go and make disciples of many nations baptizing them in the name of the Father, the Son, and the Holy Spirit while teaching them all that God has commanded you!"*

~ Matthew 28:19,20 (paraphrased)

Believing in Jesus is the first step. Accepting Him as Lord and Savior is the next step. Whenever you believe in who He is and what He has done, you accept Him as your King and are willing to stand up for Him. The way to do this is by "taking up your cross and following Him."

In order to take up your cross and follow Him you must leave behind people, places, and things. You must remove all things that stand in the way of truly following Him. If you say a "sinners prayer", you may have prayed a prayer that asked God to forgive you for your sins and invited Him into your life, but did you **truly** mean it? We previously went over "faith without works is dead." Therefore, a faithful prayer without faithful actions that follow results in a meaningless walk. A meaningless walk is not a walk that resembles Christ. Disciples are those who are active in their faith and their actions resemble the character of Christ. Jesus was meek, meaning He controlled His strength and disciplined Himself. He treated people with care, gentleness, and compassion. He gave His life up as a true servant rather than demanding others to serve Him as their God. He endured suffering when He didn't have to, but because it was His Father's will. He faced the opposition of religious people. He faced the evil of a fallen world. He was on a mission and it became accomplished! He was very fierce, tenacious, and bold. He was faithful and not fearful. He was full of love and integrity. This is the character we are to follow. We are to seek out a discovery for His entire character and pray the characteristic traits are added into our own lives. Jesus told His disciples they must give up everything, deny themselves, and take up their cross to follow Him.

"And if you do not carry your own cross and follow Me, you cannot be My disciple."

~ Luke 14:27

"So you cannot become My disciple without giving up everything you own."

~ Luke 14:33

"If you cling to your life you will lose it, but if you give it up for Me you will find it."

~ Luke 17:33

"And if you do not carry your own cross and follow Me you are not worthy of being Mine. If you cling to your life you will lose it, but if you give it up for Me you will find it."

~ Matthew 10:38,39

"Then Jesus said to His disciples, 'If any of you wants to be My follower, you must turn from your selfish ways, take up your cross, and follow Me. If you try to hang on to your life, you will lose it. But, if you give your life up for My sake, you will save it."

~ Matthew 16:24,25

"Then, calling the crowd to join His disciples, He said, 'If any of you wants to be My follower, you must turn from your selfish ways, take up your cross, and follow Me. If you try to hang on to your life, you will lose it. But if you give up your life for My sake and for the sake of the Good News, you will save it."

~ Mark 8:34,35

"Then He said to the crowd, 'If any of you wants to be My follower, you must turn from your selfish ways, take up your cross daily, and follow Me. If you try to hang on to your life, you will lose it. But if you give up your life for My sake, you will save it. And what do you benefit if you gain the whole world but are yourself lost or destroyed? If anyone is ashamed of Me and My message, the Son of Man will be ashamed of that person when He returns in His glory and in the glory of the Father and the holy angels. I tell you the truth, some standing here right now will not die before they see the Kingdom of God."

~ Luke 9:23-27

Seven scriptures later, we are given clear direction as to what we should do. We are to carry our own cross and follow Jesus. We must give up things that stand in our way for doing such. We must give up our old ways of living and embark on the new journey God has in store for us. The new life sure beats the old life. Your life may be awesome and if it is, great! It only gets better. God does not tell us to give up our lives for a lesser life. He challenges us to give up our lesser lives for ABUNDANT LIFE!

"The thief comes to steal, kill, and destroy. But I have come to give abundant life."

~ John 10:10

As we take up our cross we are reminded of Jesus every moment of our lives because we carry a cross on our back that consistently reminds us of Who we are living for. This little reminder empowers us to take the Good News in numerous places, lands distant and lands also near. We are challenged to make disciples of many nations. "Of" many nations refers to people from all over. America is a melting pot of people from all over. African Americans are "of" many nations.

Many Caucasians are also "of" many nations since they are maybe Scottish, Dutch, and German or Irish and French. Either way, all of us Gentiles are "of" many nations. Make disciples where you are at today! Become discipled first, though, to train yourself for the task.

"Work hard to present yourself to God and receive His approval. Be a good worker, one who needs not to be ashamed, and who correctly explains the Word of Truth."

~2 Timothy 2:15

"For I am not ashamed of the Good News of Christ. It is the power of God at work, saving everyone who believes- the Jew first and also the Gentile."

~ Romans 1:16

We are to carry our cross, follow Jesus, understand the truth, spread the Gospel, and never be ashamed of what He has called us to do!

Jesus is not a weak God begging for you to accept Him! He is a fierce, tenacious, and bold God challenging you to man up or woman up so you may follow Him into the unknown. He has paved the way to being raised to new life, conquering death, and reining in Heaven. The best way to get to Heaven is to "follow Him." Don't just pray a "sinners prayer."

"LIFE IS A BEAUTIFUL GIFT. JESUS HELPS US UNWRAP THE GIFT TO FIND ITS CORE BEAUTY."

~ TY FORD

CHAPTER 10:
The Power of Words

In the book of James, where Jesus's half-brother wrote about the power of the tongue, he referred to it as a "tiny rudder of a ship", controlling the ships entire direction as to where it would go. We control where we go in life with our tongue alone.

You sit down at a restaurant and order your food by what you speak. If you want your grits with cheese but don't tell them you want cheese on it you obviously won't get what you want. If you're a producer of a play and you don't give great instructions to the performers you won't get a great performance.

Life is real simple once we decide to actually break it all down. God spoke the entire universe into existence but how did He do this? Well, if you break down "universe," you find that "uni" means one, and "verse" means statement. Therefore, God spoke the universe into existence in simply "one statement." Now, that's powerful!

What are you speaking into existence today? Or, better yet what do you choose to speak into existence?

You see, the choice is yours. You can either speak positive things into existence or on the contrary, negative things. In other words, we either speak "life" or "death" in every little thing we say. It's not simply what we say, but also how we say it and for what purpose we are saying it.

Ask yourself when you say things, "Why did I say that, how did I say that, and what was the purpose for saying it?" Life is beautiful. People are beautiful. People can also be mean at times but for those little moments where imperfect people in a fallen world say something so positive, full of life and truth, it is absolutely beautiful!

"So God created human beings in His own image. In the image of God He created them; male and female He created them."

~ Genesis 1:27

So, if God created us in His very own image isn't it safe to say we have power in the words we speak since He spoke the universe into existence by what He said in simply one statement alone? The answer is, "yes!" So, what are you going to say today? You obviously have not a clue, but you can become determined in an essence to dedicate each day to speaking life into your own life and in others' lives as well. You may speak positive things into your life and positive things in other people's lives as well.

Speaking words into this air linger around and travel around in such a way that is beyond what we can possibly fathom. You may say something to a friend like, "Did you know that I love you and accept you just the way you are? Not only that but I also know someone else who loves you and accepts you beyond my capability with impeccable power and His name is Jesus. He died just for you. For one moment, you were all that was on His mind and He followed through with His death because of you but later raised from the dead, conquering death! He will give you a better life that will last forever constantly getting better along the way!" Say that at your next bus stop and let your heart feel the presence of victory while your imagination attempts to fathom how far those words traveled!

Life is a beautiful gift. Jesus helps us unwrap the gift to find its core beauty. His Word is not to beat us up but to lift us up! It gives us the tools we need to live a better life. If we didn't have His Word we wouldn't be aware of all that we need to be aware of. Are you well aware? Or, have you not read the instructions?

I encourage you today to find a 1 year reading plan and begin today. Be dedicated to reading that one little day's worth every single day. You will then prosper!

"Study this Book of Instruction continually. Meditate on it day and night so you will be sure to obey everything written in it. Only then will you prosper and succeed in all you do."

Joshua 1:8 NLT

Sunsets are beautiful and they are hard to describe. You can allow me to tell you about a sunset or you can drive down there before it's too late and see for yourself. Think about what watching a beautiful sunset does to you. Times that by about a billion and that's what the Word of God does. It reveals things to us that we could not see before. Before I was blinded, but now I can see. The Word of God binds blindness giving us enough sight to see the light. Once you have read the Word of God relentlessly and with dedication, you will find your own language to have become in line with His words. Eventually, you will be talking just like Jesus but with your own unique personality to give it all a special flavor. His Word inspires the words I speak. They have given me a great direction with peaceful sailing. I don't get in arguments with people over stupid things. I really don't argue with anyone anymore. I believe what I believe and have a clear understanding as to what it is I believe. If someone asks me to tell them what I believe, how I believe, or why I believe; I will be honest with them and speak from my heart. If they want to argue, I won't argue back. I will simply explain to them that they asked me a question and I answered it sincerely. Some people can only take truth in small doses before they can swallow the whole pill. I could only take a small dose here and there at first, but eventually I fell in love with the truth and have continued to discover more and more truth every day.

Aren't you tired of hearing the world's lies? I sure was. I was sick and tired of being sick and tired. I was sick and tired of hearing lies, speaking lies, and my own life being a living lie. Treat yourself to the truth every day by whatever dose it is you choose to indulge. Some days I only read one verse, but that verse travels with me throughout the entire day and typically longer than that.

"Above all, you must realize that no prophecy in Scripture ever came from the prophet's own understanding, or from human initiative. No, those prophets were moved by the Holy Spirit, and they spoke from God."

~2 Peter 1:20, 21

The great thing about New Living Translation is that it tells you the meaning of each verse with easy comprehension. For Fourth Day Ministries, we give away Tyndale Life Application Study Bibles in this translation. We, at Fourth Day Ministries, find this to be the easiest to understand. We typically give away Bibles with a leatherback cover because we feel that an eternal gift must be something exquisite and in perfect condition. The truth of the matter is the world today is attracted by what they see and the majority of people do take into strong consideration the looks of any book or anything.

If you need a Bible like this or know someone else who does please feel free to email me at:

fourthdayministries@gmail.com

To donate, visit our website at:

fourthdayministries.org

2 Peter 1:20, 21 tells us where the Word of God comes from. It comes from God but has been written by man with God's anointing. The best way to prove the truth of God's Word is by its sovereignty. For example, look at Isaiah 53:4-7, John 3:16, and Mark 15:37-39.

"Yet it was our weaknesses He carried; it was our sorrows that weighed Him down. And we thought His troubles were a punishment from God, a punishment for His own sins! But He was pierced for our rebellion, crushed for our sins. He was beaten so we could be whole. He was whipped so we could be healed. All of us,

like sheep, have strayed away. We have left God's paths to follow our own. Yet The Lord laid on Him the sins of us all. He was oppressed and treated harshly, yet He never said a word. He was led like a lamb to the slaughter. And as a sheep is silent before the shearers, He did not open His mouth."

~ Isaiah 53:4-7

In other words, Isaiah was "prophesying" Jesus' death from approximately 700 years prior. He went on to explain the significance of His death even. He presents Jesus' death as a perfect sacrifice for an imperfect world where people who are sinners may recognize as a gift. God used Isaiah in this matter to pull aside the curtain of time to let the people of Isaiah's day look ahead to the perfect sacrifice for man's sins, Jesus Christ and His Crucifixion.

Then, tie Isaiah 53:4-7 to John 3:16!

"For God so loved the world that He gave His only Son so that everyone who believes in Him will not perish but have eternal life."

~ John 3:16

Jesus is telling Nicodemus, who was a well-respected Jewish teacher, that in order for a man to be saved he must be born again. Nicodemus was wondering how that was possible and in John 3:16, Jesus tells him that believing in the Son of God is the ticket to Heaven. So if Isaiah tells us that, "He was beaten so we could be whole," we must understand then that God was sending someone to save us. Then, in John 3:16 we see that we must believe in Jesus Christ for us to have eternal life. The best form of "belief" is "acceptance." I do not only believe in Jesus Christ, but I better yet "accept" Him as my Lord and Savior. Furthermore, when you accept Christ, you take up your cross and follow Christ. Carrying your cross and following Jesus is what obedience consists of.

Your obedience will bear fruit for God's Kingdom and impact the lives of others in a major way! The death Isaiah prophesied about and the offering from God of His Son as the perfect sacrifice all ties together with this last scripture.

"Then Jesus uttered another loud cry and breathed His last. And the curtain in the sanctuary of the Temple was torn in two, from top to bottom. When the Roman officer who stood facing Him saw how He had died, he exclaimed, "This man truly was the Son of God!"

~ Mark 15:37-39

Hallelujah! The sovereignty of God ties together everything with full meaning, truth, and reliability. It all ties together. His entire Word works this way. There's many more examples I can show you but this book is to give you an idea of God, His power, and the truth of Jesus and His teachings. There is "Sovereignty with Christ" because He is all mighty and powerful who heals our brokenness and shapes us up into a total new creature that we are happy to see in the mirror every morning before breakfast and devotion.

God raised me from the dirt ever since I accepted Christ! I became raised from a dead man into a total transformed man with a peace that has moved mountains for me. Jesus Christ is the way. He is the truth. And He is the life. I love this life! I love the truth! This life came from God. He let me try and make it on my own, but I couldn't. It is truly a blessing to have survived all the near death experiences I encountered to have made it to where I am today. If I lose everything tomorrow I will still have Jesus and for me, that's enough.

What kind of life do you choose to have? Are you willing to give God a shot? That's all I did and boy oh boy... It has been quite the ride and experience! These words we speak are so powerful because look at what God's Word has done. He made us to be like Him. I want to be just like Jesus. And one day I will be! Today I am pretty close. I am way closer to being like Him now than I used to be. That's for sure!

God used people nearly a thousand years before Christ walked the earth for giving people a hope such as the promise of Christ's coming. He can use you today to tell people of the significance in Christ's Second Coming. God's Word has nearly 2,000 prophecies by means of over 8,000 verses. Can we say sovereignty? Jesus is a Man of His Word and if He says He is coming back then guess what? Gear up and be ready because He's surely coming!

Matthew 28:19, 20 tells us to **"Go and make disciples of many nations!"** You may say, "Many nations? How on earth am I supposed to do that?" Start with where you're at today and see where God takes you from there. Let God be the pilot.

Our tongue may be like a tiny rudder of a ship controlling where it goes but if God is the pilot of our tongue, what we say will count and we will be headed in the right direction. Then, also guess what... So will other people because of what we say. What we say matters. Make every word count! Look for the inner beauty of a person, then as you discover that inner beauty the outer appearance will have improved so much you can't help but notice how gorgeous their heart is. Do people act up and get out of line from time to time? Of course! We all do.

But, let's not come against each other because of it. Light overpowers darkness and every person has light in them, regardless of whether it really shows just yet or not. It's there and as long as we nurture that light, it will grow; and before long the darkness will have gone away to hide. Trust me. What I write is out of experience. I will not write anything in this book unless I have full confidence in the message that is being delivered! We are living in a fallen world and it sure could use some good words. It sure could use some good words to deliver life amongst it. There are not many people at all in today's world that are "comfortable" to share their faith with others. My suggestion is to do it anyways because guess what? I have and it works!

Sovereignty of Christ

The valuable lesson I have learned through my growth is that those in darkness do not want to be preached to but they sure could use some love. When people see that you love and care for them they will be willing to listen to just about anything you tell them. Your words are important. They matter. God used His Words to create the universe and because He made us in His own image we have the same "type" of power. We too can create an awesome atmosphere. Try it at work. Try it at home. Try it out in public. Try it with your friends. Try it everywhere and watch what happens but remember, you won't ever "see" just how far those words travel. But, have faith and know that they sure do travel quite the distance changing the world into a better environment and a better place.

CHAPTER 11:
Joy of Living for Christ

I never knew what to expect from joy until I gave my life to Christ. I was able to force myself to be happy in the midst of suffering, because how miserable I was happened to be funny to me at the time. But, I never knew what joy was. Joy is something that must be experienced in order to comprehend.

Joy comes from living for Christ! A sunset can be explained only to a small extent in comparison to its fullness of mesmerizing beauty when actually seen. The same goes for joy. I will do my best here to explain it to the point where it will pique your curiosity enough for you to strive towards experiencing it for yourself.

I did drugs because I was intrigued by the stories others shared with me from their experiences. But once I tried them, I did them because I liked the feeling. I have never been so high until I began living for Christ. The high is so good that it gives me not only joy, but also peace and love as well. There ain't no high like the Most High!

Last night I walked outside, sat down in a chair, and stared at the sky just to talk to God and have fellowship with Him. I looked up at first and I could only see a glimpse of what all was actually there. Then, as I talked with Him more He began to reveal things to me through the sky. The clouds began to change their form in the area I could see because of the moonlight. They all changed so quickly and before I knew it I could see a giant face that I clearly comprehended as God presenting Himself to me. Might sound crazy, but a lot of what I talk about in this spiritual journey sounds crazy; however, once you actually experience it for yourself, you will understand. God is pretty wild. I enjoy having a wild, great time and God gives me that as a gift every single day. Those clouds I saw were God's way of speaking to me as I had fellowship with Him. After I saw the face, everything began to expand and that all signified to me just how big God is! It was clear that my eyes could not possibly see Him all at once. I saw these crazy rigid clouds in bulk that to me were on the other side of the moon representing the numerous angels God sends my way every single day to secure my safety and protection.

This is simply one of many personal interactions with God that I have had. I felt so much joy and overwhelming peace from it all that it blew my mind! Philippians 4:4-8 talks about a peace that is indescribable and the Scripture tells us what it takes to find this peace. When I have peace, it opens the door for joy and love. When I have joy I have peace and when I have both of those, love is always included. Verses 4-8 says,

"Always be full of joy in The Lord. I say it again- rejoice. Let everyone see that you are considerate in all you do. Remember, The Lord is coming soon. Don't worry about anything. Instead, pray about everything. Tell God what you need and thank Him for all He has done. If you do this, you will experience God's peace which is far more wonderful than the human mind can understand. His peace will guard your hearts and minds as you live in Christ Jesus. And now, dear brothers and sisters let me say one more thing before I close this letter. Fix your thoughts on what is true and honorable and right. Think about things that are pure, lovely, and admirable. Think about things that are excellent and worthy of praise."

~ Philippians 4:4-8

Notice, when you're always full of joy in The Lord, peace that surpasses understanding is also near. His peace and joy can take away our worries. Praying helps lift our burdens. Thinking positive helps us maintain the peace and joy that prevents us from drowning in worry.

We praise God when we are full of joy because of Him! When we walk around with such joy we are able to be considerate in just about all that we do. This joy ought to never leave us when we keep in mind that Jesus is coming back! One day, He will be here to bring judgement on this world and hopefully you will have already been raptured up into Heaven before then. But when He comes back, those of us who have been taken up will be coming back behind Him and His glory as He leads the way back into this world to reveal Himself ! We do not need to worry about anything at all! It is wise to prepare ahead for each day and by doing that it will help alleviate most of our worries.

Our worries are actually sinful because it represents our lack of trust for God and His will. Being concerned about some things is okay because that's a healthy way of having an awareness for all that is going on. Worrying is just foolish in the eyes of God because He is always in control and whatever happens in our lives, good or bad, He will turn around for the good (Romans 8:28 reference). He will turn around for the good when we prove our love to Him by obedience. As soon as we begin to obey God. He begins to turn things around for the good immediately!

Jesus says if we love Him, obey His commandments (John 14:15). Therefore, when we obey The Lord because we truly love Him, He will begin to shift things in such a way that they work together for the good. God is in control. However, mankind has free will that God's control can't necessarily overturn.

God can turn things around for the good when our free will chooses obedience and aligns itself with His will. We all need some things to happen and nearly all of those things require prayer. It is better to pray for what we need rather than worrying about whether or not our needs will be given to us. Come boldly to the Throne and tell our Savior what it is you need and thank Him for all that He has already given to you. We have the luxury of being supplied by God according to His glorious riches in Christ Jesus (Philippians 4:19 reference).

Sovereignty of Christ

We also have the performance capabilities in this earth as human beings like that of a Bugatti sports car on an advanced race track. We have this performance because of Christ Jesus and His part in our lives. We "can" do all things through Him because He strengthens us so we can do everything we need to do in this Christian walk here on earth (Philippians 4:13).

Our actions are not intended to be rooted in performance, but rooted in love. God wants sincere disciples and not actors that fake it or do things to be noticed. God looks at the heart. At the same time, when it comes to facing difficult obstacles, God gives us everything we need to rise above our circumstances and overcome. We are more than conquerors through Christ Jesus (Romans 8:37).

The peace God gives with all this kind of knowledge will most definitely blow your mind, or should I say "surpass your understanding." Such peace will surely guard your hearts and minds. Your heart can be sturdy and strong with such a fire field of protection around it like this peace. Your mind can be protected from the fiery darts of the enemy that want to infiltrate it with horrible thoughts and tendencies to cause worries. Ephesians 6 talks about the helmet of salvation protecting our minds in the same kind of way. So, the best way to protect your mind is to tell God what you need and thank Him for all He has done after putting on your helmet of salvation. Then, help protect your heart by strapping on the "breastplate of righteousness." I literally just put my whole armor on because I want security, peace, love, and joy. I also want the performance to operate in such a way that leads others to Christ! Go ahead and throw it all on yourself from top to bottom. Start with helmet of salvation. Then, breastplate of righteousness, shield of faith, sword of the Spirit which is the Word of God, belt of truth, and shoes which are sandaled for the readiness of Gospel of Peace (Ephesians 6 reference).

Once you do all this and "fix" your thoughts on honorable truth and righteousness, you will find yourself living life with an entirely renewed perspective.

Our perspective that we choose to have can develop a totally new reality for us. I don't know about you, but I needed a totally new reality to better the way I saw things in this world. What is pure, lovely, and admirable will always profit us much more than focusing on imperfections and frustrations. That's life verses death and positive verses negative. That's upside right instead of upside down. I can notice your imperfections and complain about them or I can look at the gifts God has given you. I could also notice your imperfections and help you conquer them by helping you use the gifts God has given you.

Light overtakes darkness. When you flip on a light switch there is no battle that takes place between the light coming on and the room staying dark. The light immediately travels across that room. Now, that's excellent and worthy of praise! Joy gives us strength!,

"Then he said to them, 'Go your way. Eat the fat and drink sweet wine and send portions to anyone who has nothing ready, for this day is holy to our Lord. And do not be grieved, for the joy of the Lord is your strength.'"

~ Nehemiah 8:10

Do not be grieved or "do not worry" because the joy of The Lord is your strength! When we are able to defeat our worries by trusting in The Lord will all our hearts, joy is granted. When we have that kind of joy we are strong and ready to conquer anything.

"Trust in The Lord with all your heart. Lean not on your own understanding. Acknowledge Him in all ways and He will direct your path."

~ Proverbs 3:5-6

God gives us direction but not until we give His Spirit the "permission" to give us that "direction."

"So he brought his people out with joy, his chosen ones with singing."

~ Psalm 105:43

When God brought me out of my own mess and turned my whole mess into a ministry, I discovered the joy I want everyone on earth to have.

"Many are called but few are chosen."

~ Matthew 22:14

We are all called. God had tried reaching me every day of my life for years but it wasn't until I heard him and answered to that call that I became "chosen." It requires an "answer" to a call to be chosen for that purpose.

"God works through different men in different ways but it is the same God who achieves His purposes through them all."

~1 Corinthians 12:6

We all have a purpose that ties into everyone else's purpose for being here. All these purposes have been ordained by God for the sake of His Kingdom. Once you realize you have been chosen you will be singing a song in your heart all the time and sometimes even out loud maybe. Possibly in Wal-Mart!

Discovering what you have been put on earth for and following through with that purpose gives you a joy that is indescribable!

We all mess up from time to time. I am not dominated by sin anymore but I do still sin from time to time (Romans 6 & Romans

138

3:23,24 reference). What do we do when we mess up? How do we go on to continue and receive that joy we once first felt?

"For if we confess our sins to Him, He is faithful and just to forgive us and cleanse us from every wrong."

~ 1 John 1:9

God wants to forgive us 24/7. Look at what lengths He went to so we could have forgiveness as an option. He died on the Cross for us and didn't say a word as He got brutally bruised and beaten! He didn't have to go through with it but out of obedience to the Father, Jesus chose to willingly die for us. He wanted to restore the fellowship between God and man that the fall of man disrupted. He wanted to redeem what was lost! And He did. Will you let Him redeem and restore you?

"Restore to me the joy of your salvation, and make me willing to obey you."

~ Psalm 51:12

This was shortly after David had committed adultery with Bathsheba. David had sent her husband off to war on the front line to purposely die so he could have her all to himself. David was a man after God's own heart and he even was a murderer and adulterer. But, neither of those sins were too big for God to forgive him of and cleanse him from the stains they caused him. Unconfessed sins cause our intimacy with God to be very distant. But, when we confess our sins to Him, intimacy is restored. He literally wipes our sins away and cleanses us from the pain they caused.

"As far as the east is from the west, so far has He removed our transgressions from us."

~ Psalm 103:12

139

David obviously wrote this but it was inspired by God for him to write it. The entire Bible has been written by God's Spirit. Remember, in Chapter 10 we went over all the prophecies in the Bible that proved its sovereignty. God is sovereign. Are you ready to be complete and fulfilled with having Christ in your life and learning how to live for Christ more and more each and every day? Give it a shot and you can't possibly go wrong! Fulfillment is like never having to take another sip of water ever again because your thirst has been forever quenched!

The wise men saw a sign that signified Jesus the Messiah had been born. This immediately gave them great joy!

"When they saw the star, they were filled with joy."

~ Matthew 2:10

They had seen a star in the east that guided them to the birthplace of Jesus, Bethlehem. They offered gifts of gold, frankincense, and myrrh. Frankincense and myrrh are prized for their alluring fragrance. These wise men offered many gifts of some prized possessions. This signifies just how joyful they really were to see Jesus. What are you willing to give to Jesus? What He wants most is to offer your body as a holy and living sacrifice to Him (Romans 12:1 reference).

He wants to use your body as a living vessel for Him and His purposes. Once you accept that and actually follow through with it, you will have this indescribable joy I speak of.

Can you imagine finding an empty grave or tomb of someone you loved and then that person appearing to you in physical form on your way to tell everyone? This happened with Mary Magdalene and the other Mary (not Jesus' mom) when they went to visit Jesus' tomb.

"So they departed quickly from the tomb with fear and great joy, and ran to tell his disciples. And behold, Jesus met them and said, 'Greetings!' And they came up and took hold of his feet and worshiped him. Then Jesus said to them, 'Do not be afraid; go and tell my brothers to go to Galilee, and there they will see me.'"

~ Matthew 28:8-10

Jesus gave these women a joy I can't even imagine! Jesus gives me indescribable joy already enough as it is. I can't even imagine what it would be like if I clearly saw Him for myself in physical form!

There are truly benefits out of this world for being a disciple for Christ. In the Old Testament under the old covenant, God used the priests of Israel to stand between the people and Him as His intercessors. But, under the new covenant all believers are like priests of The Lord.

We, as believers, are the intercessors between God and unbelievers.

"Instead of shame and dishonor, you will enjoy a double share of honor. You will possess a double portion of prosperity in your land, and everlasting joy will be yours."

~ Isaiah 61:7

Prosperity, joy, and honor sound much better than shame and dishonor. What a trade!? Therefore, following Christ's footsteps by ministering to those in the world profits yourself as well. I say that because I want you to understand how putting God and others first will not cause you to go out of your way for no reason. It will surely pay off for you as well! There is not a paycheck of any amount that can compare with God's payments for your obedience! We reap what we sow and no matter how much you sow God will outdo you every time by what you reap.

Obviously, ministering to the world takes a strategic plan and cannot be done out of foolishness. I learned the hard way how easy it was to beat someone over the head with the Bible, but that doesn't work. I soon figured out my walk would speak for itself. This is a much better tool which causes others to send the invitation to me in middle of conversation. My walk alone opens the door for explaining and sharing the teachings of Christ that I have learned. We must always have both ears open and neither eyes closed. There are plenty of opportunities in everyday life to share the Good News with others because everybody must know, "God's not Dead but He is surely Alive!"

Proverbs are considered the "book of wisdom."

"An evil man is ensnared in his transgression, but a righteous man sings and rejoices."

~ Proverbs 29:6

A righteous man sings and rejoices because he is full of joy! An evil man is held captive by his own sins. They are actually ropes that catch and hold him back (Proverbs 5:21,22 reference). I would much rather be joyful because of my righteousness than shameful because of a heavy conscience from my evildoings.

We are righteous in God's sight simply by our faith in Jesus Christ and understanding the significance of what He did at the Cross. It is "accepting" the gift of eternal life that sets us free. Once we understand that, we want to live a better life out of gratitude for what the Cross stands for. The Holy Spirit helps us live the better life we desire. Ephesians 1:13 tells us that we receive the Holy Spirit after believing in Jesus Christ. Paul here says:

"And now you Gentiles have also heard the truth, the Good News that God saves you. And when you believed in Christ, He identified you as His own by giving you the Holy Spirit, whom He promised long ago."

~ Ephesians 1:13

The Holy Spirit is God's guarantee that we are His and that He will do what He promises all the time.

"You haven't done this before. Ask, using my name, and you will receive, and you will have abundant joy."

~ John 16:24

These are actually Jesus' words. Remember, He is a Man of His word and this Man is indeed God.

"He despises those whom God rejects but honors those who obey The Lord. He always does what He promises no matter how much it may cost."

~ Psalm 15:4

So whatever you want, ask in Jesus' name and you will receive. However, it must be in line with His will. Once you receive whatever it is you asked for, abundant joy is all yours!

Experience the joy of living for Christ today! Enjoy it tomorrow! Enjoy it for the rest of your life! Share it with others and receive even more!

"WE ARE RIGHTEOUS IN GOD'S SIGHT SIMPLY BY OUR FAITH IN JESUS CHRIST AND UNDERSTANDING THE SIGNIFICANCE OF WHAT HE DID AT THE CROSS."

~TY FORD

CHAPTER 12:
Wisdom & Spiritual Warfare

In my life, I have experienced consequences from opposing sides of contrary actions.

In other words, I have made some bad choices and suffered the bad consequences from those actions. That was much of what my life was like growing up. Some call it growing pains. In reality, it is simply sin. There are more definitions to "wisdom" than just one. Wisdom can simply be defined by "recognizing the future consequences of present choices, good or bad."

If I procrastinate writing this chapter, I may not be able to reach someone this chapter is meant for. If I don't take out the trash on Tuesday and they pick up trash every Wednesday and Saturday, my garbage will become overloaded and the neighborhood dogs may just have their way with my garbage, leaving a mess in my driveway. If I take the trash out, the good consequences for that action are avoiding a mess to clean up.

The consequences for our everyday lives don't always affect "just" us directly. Sometimes they affect us indirectly and others around us directly. For example, if you see a homeless person and feel led by God to drop them a few bucks but don't, it affects them directly but you still reap an uneasy heart. When something is put on your heart to do out of love for someone else it is meant to directly affect that person but it will also affect you too.

When I feel led to pray for somebody and don't, I feel like I disobeyed God. Then I think, "what if I had prayed for them? What would have happened? How could that have made a difference?"

Sovereignty of Christ

A life lived for God is full of excitement and truly a "rush!" God puts some crazy things on my heart for me to do and they are always so unusual and out of the ordinary! But, when I do them, I become blessed for doing them, and as a result for my obedience someone else is helped. Those are the good consequences I tend to reap for doing what is put on my heart by God for me to do.

The adversary, the devil, the little punk that lost the keys to his own home, will do his best job to deceive us and confuse us enough for us to do something he wishes for us to do. He will cause you to think that smoking a joint will ease your mind. He will cause you to think that alcohol in excess will solve all your problems. He will make you really believe that having sex with someone out of wedlock is the way to express your love for that special someone. He will make you feel like getting mad and yelling obscene words will unleash the tension in your mind. He will make you want to believe the lies instead of the truth. He will twist your perspective to cause "strife" between you and your co-workers or maybe between you and your family. Strife is drama and tension that causes division between a group of people.

God is a God of unity while the devil is His opponent that will do everything he possibly can in order to interfere with the unity that is of God's will. When I worked at Mercy House Ministries, that little punk (the devil) would twist all sorts of things up! He would make it look like one staff member was selling drugs to some students. He would cause people to hear "one" thing that would lead them to a false conclusion instead of hearing the "whole" thing which would have led them to the truth. Then, once I became fully dedicated to Fourth Day Ministries that little punk would try to twist up conversation between my dad and I so that we would be in strife. Note that Fourth Day Ministries is a family project while my dad is the President and I am the Founder and Pastor. The rest of our family are full of ideas, support, and advice. My wife is the women's leader of the ministry.

"The wisdom that comes from Heaven is first of all pure and full of quiet gentleness. Then it is peace, loving, and courteous. It allows discussion and is willing to yield to others; it is full of mercy and good deeds. It is wholehearted, straightforward, and sincere."

~James 3:17

Notice that the Word says this wisdom comes from Heaven. The wisdom my dad and I have is not wisdom we were born with or wisdom we inherited from the world. No, this wisdom is that in which comes from God and since Jesus Christ died for us and left us with the Holy Spirit after He ascended into Heaven, we have His wisdom!

The devil tries to trip us up but we are able to see what is really going on. This is because of our discernment which also is a gift from God. After I preach the Word and write some chapters for the Kingdom of God, here comes that nasty little punk. I am waiting for him every time because he shows up after we do something spectacular for God. I had to simply get off the phone with my dad one time to cool down and had to call him back the next day to apologize while also the both of us recognized what had really happened. Neither one of us were upset with each other but mad about how bad the devil caused the conversation to spiral out of control. The devil would cause us to "react" instead of "respond." We both knew what was going on and the devil will not be tolerated in interfering with the relationships I have with others.

My life is a battle as the devil is constantly fighting me to deceive me and doubt my purpose for the Kingdom of God. But, guess who's on my side? God and His army. We just can't be stopped! Take that devil! Whose side are you on? Are you willing to make wise choices and reap good consequences? Recognize that bad choices reap bad consequences leading to a state of misery.

The devil is miserable and he wants your company. But, God is a good God who made you to be an awesome person and He died not for "all of us," but for "each of us!" He is Lord and Savior over your life when you enter into relationship with Him after you decide to accept Him and commit yourself to obeying Him. He died for all. However, He wants to get to know each of us on an intimate and personal level. For just one moment you were all that was on His mind. He is so sovereign and loving that instead of Him fighting back He didn't say a word as He chose to think about every man and woman that ever lived or ever would live so that He really could make that moment in His life count. For in those moments, He has given us the opportunity to receive through Him the security of eternal life in His presence. What an awesome God!

You see, the wisdom that comes from the world is "foolishness" in the eyes of God. I have learned to see things from God's point of view as a result of me always praying for it. Wisdom can be also defined by, "Learning to see life from God's perspective. Recognizing a cause and effect relationship in life. Tracing conflicts to their root causes. Learning how to apply principles of life to daily situations. Discerning between natural inclinations and false philosophies and rejecting them." What I had to do when my dad and I's conversation spiraled out of control was ask myself, "What is the root cause to this conflict?"

The answer was spiritual warfare.

There is so much spiritual warfare going on right now all around you as you read this book. If you could see it you would probably pass out because it would be pretty freaky!

Ephesians 6 tells us what to do about this spiritual warfare, though. It tells us to guard ourselves from this spiritual warfare by putting on the helmet of salvation, breastplate of righteousness, shield of faith, sword of the Spirit which is the Word of God, belt of truth, and shoes which are sandaled for the readiness of the Gospel of Peace. The helmet of salvation protects us from the fiery darts that the enemy shoots at us in hopes of penetrating our mind with evil. The breastplate of righteousness is for us to always be confident in our righteousness and secure in our identity. Our righteousness comes from our faith in what Jesus did at the Cross. He died for us and by us believing in Him and accepting the gift of eternal life that comes through Him, we are righteous in God's sight. The shield of faith shields us from all fear and helps us move the mountains that stand in our way so we may reach the victory that awaits us. The sword of the Spirit is the Word of God and is referred to as a "sword" because of its powerful capabilities.

Jesus Christ in the wilderness defeated the devil with the Word of God. He was attacked by the devil in three ways: pride of life, lust of the flesh, and lust of the eyes. The devil tried to use God's own Word against Him but failed because Christ knew exactly what the Word really said. Rat poison is so deadly to rats because it's not all poison. It is also food which lures the rats in to eat it. Satan in the garden twisted the truth just enough to trip up Eve. Satan changed God's words of "You will die" to "You won't die." Satan changed just one word to deceive Eve which led to the sin of both Adam and Eve. Rat poison contains mostly food with a small percentage of poison but enough poison to kill a rodent. Satan twisted the Word of God enough to cause the statement to be in line with what God had said by 2/3 words. Satan used one word to flip the whole thing upside down.

Wisdom protects us from deception. The Word of God is most powerful in those people who are most familiar with it. The shoes that are sandaled for carrying the Gospel to others brings peace to those near and far. This armor that you put on every day or "should" put on every day will change the way you endure circumstances. Wisdom can break down a conflict and turn it into triumph. That is, "wisdom that comes from Heaven."

"Stop deceiving yourselves. If you think you are wise by the world's standards, you need to become a fool to be truly wise. For the wisdom of this world is foolishness to God. As the Scriptures say, 'He traps the wise in the snares of their own cleverness."

~1 Corinthians 3:18,19

149

Paul here is explaining how the wisdom that we see in great messengers comes from God. Paul exclaims the importance of placing trust in God alone and not the man.

I can be only so smart on my own but with the Holy Spirit and His wisdom which comes from Heaven, the sky is not even the limit for such wisdom. This universe has been designed in such a way where consequences, both good and bad, have been implemented into its structure. My actions reap consequences every time. All actions are either good or bad. Some actions may be good, but because of the spiritual warfare that goes on, those actions wage war with the enemy which cause him to strike back and maybe influences something bad to happen. The enemy only has the power of "suggestion," which is a form of "influence." He is a master negotiator! Do not fear though because, "God causes everything to work together for the good for those who love Him and are called according to His purpose" (Romans 8:28). When we make the devil mad we are doing something right! I preach the Gospel on Sunday and get attacked Monday. However, the Word I preached to maybe 45 people helped all 45, but I get attacked as a result of my actions being so significant for the Kingdom. Commanders are the ones the enemy wishes to strike down dead the most.

My purpose in explaining all of this is to signify how not all good actions reap good consequences alone. When you do something bold and terrific there will always be "haters" that want to bring you down. The devil is a "hater" amongst haters. The good consequences out of a result to our obedience for God will far outweigh the devil's capabilities to trip us up and cause destruction. So, understand that the good consequences will always outdo the devil's strikes back. Don't be scared or frightened of the devil. Just know that God is with you and He will be "filtering" everything that comes your way as you are in His will.

"The Lord is my light and my salvation, so why should I be afraid? The Lord protects me from danger, so why should I tremble? When evil people come to destroy me. When my enemies and foes attack me. They will stumble and fall. Though a mighty army surrounds me, my heart will know no fear. Even if they attack me, I remain confident. The one thing I ask of The Lord. The thing I seek the most is to live in the house of The Lord all the days of my life delighting in The Lord's perfections and meditating in His temple."

~ Psalm 27:1-4

Where there is "light" there is "salvation." Light overpowers darkness. Flip on a light switch and notice how the light travels across the room before darkness even has a chance to fight. There is nothing to be afraid of because of the protection and security the will of God offers us. The brain is protected inside the skull but not if you take the brain out of that skull. The brain would not be able to do its job and it would have zero protection. Are you "in" or "outside" of God's will today?

"For the reverence and fear of God are basic to all wisdom."

~ Proverbs 9:10

When I think of how I listen to someone, I recognize that if that person does not have credibility with me, I really don't listen. And, if I don't listen, I have zero chances for learning anything that person has to offer. Have I given that person a chance to earn any credibility or have I immediately jumped to the dramatic conclusion that they have nothing to offer for me? I did not want to listen to anyone talk to me about God for many years because I feared God in a way, but was unable to show Him any reverence. Since I was so close-minded to God, the person wanting to talk to me about Him had zero chances to get across any valid points to me. Now, I love Jesus Christ and choose to live for Him every day! I understand the Gospel unlike before and I am eager to hear anyone talk about Him! Now that I have "reverence" to the Father, I am able to develop wisdom

151

because of my "willingness to learn" and "teachability." I am willing to learn now out of my reverence to God which has been the very starting point to gaining wisdom.

"Get all the advice and instruction you can and be wise the rest of your life."

~ Proverbs 19:20

Once I became reverent to God I was willing to listen to other people talk about Him and deliver messages that pertained to Him. I recognize that King Solomon, David's son, was the wisest man that ever walked this earth besides Jesus Christ Himself. King Solomon was so rich and wealthy that his splendor caused a "Queen" to pass out when she visited him.

"And when the queen of Sheba had seen all the wisdom of Solomon, the house that he had built, the food of his table, the seating of his officials, and the attendance of his servants, their clothing, his cupbearers, and his burnt offerings that he offered at the house of the Lord, there was no more breath in her."

~1 Kings 10:4

There was "no more breath in her" meaning she had passed out! You have got to be pretty wealthy to cause a "Queen" to pass out as a result of her awe that your riches and splendor caused her! Queens are pretty rich themselves if you know what I mean! King Solomon was so strong because he had a wise "counsel." He did not delegate responsibilities with a thumb over his counsel-men always controlling what they did and how they did things. They would have responsibilities they were all entrusted with and they were all there for advice to help one another. Solomon accepted advice. He allowed people to counsel him even though he was extremely wise himself. I have learned that everyone has great ideas. Not all of everyone's ideas are great but everyone has a few excellent ideas. Not all great ideas work but when I take the advice and instruction from others, I am able to be stronger in wisdom than if I used only the ideas of my own. Let's face it! We are not the only ones with great ideas. If your idea is better than mine I will surely use yours; that is wisdom that is embraced with humility. In this life, I have learned that wisdom is a valuable asset to have. I also recognize that I was not at all wise in the best of my days as a sinner. However, once I accepted Christ into my heart and believed in Him to work through me, I have become wiser as a result. Furthermore, I went from being a foolish sinner to a wiser servant. God is so sovereign in the sense that He is everywhere all of the time and nothing gets past Him. God is never surprised.

Once we allow this sovereignty to be added unto our lives by inheriting His wisdom, we see the bigger picture and are able to live out our lives accordingly.

"For my thoughts are completely different from yours says The Lord. And my ways are far beyond anything you could imagine. For just as the heavens are higher than the earth, so are my ways higher than your ways and thoughts higher than your thoughts."

~ Isaiah 55:8,9

When He is living inside of us and we are in tune with what He is doing in our lives, we are able to see life from His perspective while recognizing the cause and effect relationships there are in life. We are able to see the future consequences of today's choices. Life is full of choices and if you are already saved, no your bad choices won't necessarily rob you of your salvation, but they will cause you to reap some bad consequences. Live wisely and make smart choices. Be of a sound mind by allowing a God of Sovereignty to direct you in your steps.

"WHERE THERE IS 'LIGHT' THERE IS 'SALVATION'. LIGHT OVERPOWERS DARKNESS. FLIP ON A LIGHT SWITCH AND NOTICE HOW THE LIGHT TRAVELS ACROSS THE ROOM BEFORE DARKNESS EVEN HAS A CHANCE TO FIGHT."

~TY FORD

CHAPTER 13:
Jehovah Ropheka
(The Lord Who Heals)

How many of us "really" believe in the healing power of the Almighty God?

I was skeptical of it for a long time because it is such a supernatural occurrence. To see someone go into a doctor's office one day and come home with cancer is devastating. But, to see believers of Christ to lay hands on that person the following Sunday and find out the next Monday that there is no more cancer in that person's body is absolutely amazing! Once you enter into the dimension of life that encompasses you with other believers, you encounter experiences that are literally out of this world!

I actually had planned on this chapter being postponed for later in this book but I am personally going through something right now with another family member that has had healing on my mind all last night and all this morning. Since this is the case, I am absolutely led to write this chapter today! You see, my sister Traci is my oldest of two siblings. I have two older sisters, Erin and Traci, who I both absolutely adore and cherish! They are so important to me and always have been. What is so special during these days are that every time I see them it is like a "prized moment" I share with them. Traci has two sons, Cameron and Ethan, and a loving husband named Scott Sammy Hager. Cameron is 13 years old and Ethan is just a couple years younger. These boys are so special to me just like Erin's two sons are as well. Erin has two sons named Ford and Rhett, which is short for Everett. She also has a loving husband named Dustin, whom I mostly refer to as Bubba. She does not like me calling him Bubba but Dustin doesn't mind, so I do anyway.

155

I received the news last night that my older sister had gotten a report from the doctor about there being a growth somewhere on her body. This was some disturbing news. However, I chose to trust in God's supernatural healing power. And, I was not let down because it was much later revealed that she was healed. God got all the glory! I have laid hands on some people at different times in church but also in the middle of an eye doctor's office one time to pray for them. Sometimes we would all lay hands on people in church with a disease or illness and many times we would receive an awesome report back only a few weeks after. I got eased into accepting the reality of God's supernatural power. I was in the eye doctor's office talking to an elderly lady whom was having eye problems so severe that she could hardly see. She was a believer and we were sharing our faith with one another until she asked me to keep her in my prayers because of her poor eyesight. So, I hesitated and said, "Mam, I could pray for you right now if you'd like to step outside." She said, "Oh dear, we can pray right here right now because I am not ashamed to pray in front of these people!" So, a student I had with me from Mercy House was with me and we laid hands on that lady right there and then and prayed for her to be healed. We got done praying and continued to carry on our conversation from before. Then, in mid conversation she said, "Ya'll, I can see so much better now. I thank ya'll for praying for me. I surely appreciate it!" I said, "Really!?" She was being honest, straightforward, and sincere. God has given me the discernment as gift to distinguish truth from lies. I am telling you the lady was telling the truth! Her eyes had literally lit all the way up and I could even see it in her eyes!

God is the Jehovah Ropheka, The Lord who heals. I have a friend in Meridian, Mississippi named Darren Martin that has been empowered by the Holy Spirit to lay hands on people, pray for them, and has witnessed people become healed many different times. He walks by faith in a spectacular kind of way. It is intriguing to hear his stories. I got to talking to him one day and asked him how he prays when he asks God for healing. I have come to understand from my knowledge of the Word is that healing is already in our Spirit when we have the Holy Spirit. And, Jesus Christ made all the deposits in the spiritual galaxy necessary for us to use in our walk with God on earth. All we have to do is make the "withdrawal" from the spiritual world so that it may be released in the natural (physical) world.

Imagine your bank account and all the deposits you have made in the past year. Once X amount of dollars has been deposited you can withdraw any amount within what you have deposited. Jesus Christ has deposited love, joy, peace, faithfulness, gentleness, kindness, goodness, patience, and self-control all in the spiritual world so that we may withdraw it from that spiritual world and into our physical lives. He also deposited healing, strength, might, wisdom, knowledge, understanding, power, endurance, and etc. We are able to make "withdrawals" from what all He has already deposited. We withdraw within the bounds of His deposits. What is so beautiful is that we have UNLIMITED access to it all. We can withdraw as much as we care to use. He will give us more than what we need as often as we need it. The "spiritual" world is the unseen world. The "physical" world is the seen world.

The spiritual (unseen) world "gives birth" to the physical (seen) world. The supernatural world gives birth to the natural world. This is what I had understanding of so far when I spoke with Darren Martin and listened closely to what it was he added. He pointed out to me how Peter told the man who couldn't walk to "Get up and walk in the name of Jesus." He explained to me how we have the authority of Jesus Christ and we must speak with that same authority in order to speak with dominion over sickness and death.

It makes perfect sense and lines up with the Word of God. If you think about it, when we have diet coke in a bottle and don't want diet in there but regular coke instead, what do we do? Well, first we must take the diet coke out of there. Then, we must replace it with regular coke. The same thing works for taking disease out of a physical body and replacing it with healing for that body. We bind the sickness or disease with the blood of Jesus and demand that illness to leave by speaking to it and declaring it to leave in Jesus Christ name. Then, we replace it with healing and health and thank God for having answered the prayer right there and then. We thank God for His supernatural power and praise Him every day for what He has done!

You see, another time I had a really good friend of mine whose step mother had recently been diagnosed with cancer. She had been diagnosed with cancer to an extreme, deadly degree. I prayed one night about her being healed and God had choked me all up. The Holy Spirit got a hold of me so much that it was extremely overwhelming and it caused me to weep. I wept and wept and thanked God for what I had faith He was going to do. All of a sudden I was directed to pick up a flash card and write on there what my friend was to do. I wrote a Scripture reference of 2 Chronicles 7:14 on their which says:

"Then if my people who are called by my name will humble themselves, pray, seek My face, and turn away from their wicked ways; I will hear from Heaven, will forgive their sins, and heal their land."

~2 Chronicles 7:14

When I saw my friend a week and a half later, I told him to share the scripture with his family and speak a brief message on it and declare the faith of his step mother being healed. I then told him his stepmother would be healed. God told me she would be healed. He just had me give him a flashcard with simple instructions so I did. I don't know what all happened right after that but I do know that within that same month his step mother had been healed of cancer. To this day, she is cancer free. Praise God!

As I had prayed over my sister because of the growth she has between last night and this morning, I had this same exact experience. I wept and God revealed to me that He would indeed heal her. I praised God and worshiped Him with an overwhelming joy as I completely trusted Him and His healing power. I see it being in

His will because He has revealed to me that it is. Just like I had to do something last time with my friend, I must also do something this time and that is to have everyone at Thanksgiving lay hands on my sister to pray for her. It is important for everyone in the family to stretch their faith out for that very moment so that the faith will release the healing from the supernatural and it be added into the natural for her mortal body to be cleansed and healed. That sickness must be bound by the blood of Jesus and removed from her body so that the healing and divine health may replace it in exchange.

We don't know of there being any cancer or anything but we do know that the growth should not be there. Just like we give Christ our sins and He gives us righteousness, we also give him sickness and disease for healing and health in exchange. How many of you can say, "Praise God!?" We serve a mighty God.

I tell you that God is big. Take Him outside of the box! Stop looking at your problems as if they stand above you and stare you down! Look down on your problems as you acknowledge and recognize you are a joint-heir of Christ! Everything He has, you also have access to! What is above your head is beneath His feet! Look up and see God! Above Him there is no one! He is above and beyond what we can ever fathom! But I tell you, fathom this... He is the Almighty and Powerful God! He is the only "Jehovah!" He is the only "personal God!" He loves you and cherishes you! He adores you! Whatever problem is yours He has dominion over!

He has given us everything we need to take over our problems, to overcome adversity, to overcome sickness, to defeat death just as He already has! Jesus already got off His Throne to come down here and show us how it's done! It's time for us to get off our high horses and perform the supernatural with the authority He has given to us! It is time for us to live in such a way that causes Him to stand up off His Throne and cheer us on saying, "That's my boy!...Shooooweee!" He died for not "all of us," but for "each of us!" He died for only you just one moment! We are talking about the "Sovereignty of Christ" ladies and gentleman!

Sovereignty meaning fullness and complete! He is everywhere all of the time! He thought of every man and every woman who ever lived and who ever would live individually on a personal basis because that's how sovereign our Lord is! He was a beast, is a beast, and will always be a beast forever and always! Can I get an Amen!? Can I get a shoowee!? Can I get a hallelujah!? Can I get a hoorah!? Don't do it for me but do it for the One who died for both you and me! Whooo! I get cold chills and an adrenaline rush when I get to going like that. We serve an awesome God who is worth serving every moment of every single day.

"But He was pierced for our rebellion, crushed for our sins. He was beaten so we could be whole. He was whipped so we could be *healed*."

~ Isaiah 53:5

You see that? He took a beating to make up for our rebellious ways! He was crushed for our "screw ups." He was severely beaten so we could be made whole and have sovereignty and completeness in our life because of what He has done! He was whipped by the cat of 9 tails where flesh was ripped out of His skin just so we could be "*healed*." I don't know anyone in the world who would take someone's bread crumbs in exchange for a billion dollars! But this Savior of ours takes all our iniquities and failures to give us eternal life, hope, joy, and peace! Where you find truth you also find grace. What an awesome God!?

"He said, 'If you will listen carefully to the voice of The Lord your God and do what is right in His sight, obeying His commands and keeping all His decrees, then I will not make you suffer any of the diseases I sent on the Egyptians; for I am The Lord who *heals* you.'"

~ Exodus 15:26

You see, God wants us to be healthy. Sickness and disease are not all always healed. However, even when that is not the case He will cause it all to work together for the good for those who love Him and are called according to His purpose (Romans 8:28 reference). He wants to heal us and to shield us from sickness and disease. With faith, mountains can be removed from our paths. Sickness and disease serve as an obstacle that is like a mountain in our path. The faith we have in Jesus Christ, knowledge of His Word, and understanding of the supernatural gives us the tools we need for removing these mountain like obstacles in our lives.

Chapter 4 of Philippians tells us to "not worry about anything but instead to pray about everything. To tell God what we need and thank Him for all He has done. Once we do that we will experience God's peace which surpasses all understanding." So, what do we need and what all has He done that we should thank Him for?

"Therefore I tell you, whatever you ask in prayer, believe that you have received it, and it will be yours. And whenever you stand praying, forgive, if you have anything against anyone, so that your Father also who is in heaven may forgive you your trespasses."

~ Mark 11:24, 25

It is by *believing* that we release the supernatural.

When you believe that something will happen you are unable to see, that strengthens the probability for it to be received. Not everything we want to happen and believe in will always happen simply because God sometimes has a better plan than what we want to happen

"For my thoughts are completely different from yours says The Lord. And my ways are far beyond anything you could imagine. For just as the heavens are higher than the earth, so are my ways higher than your ways and thoughts higher than your thoughts."

~ Isaiah 55:8, 9

He is always in control and what we may want to happen could be the less fortunate in comparison to what He has planned.

"He has plans to prosper us and not for evil. He has plans to give us a future and a hope."

~ Jeremiah 29:11 (paraphrased)

It is important for us to forgive others so we can be forgiven by God for everything we do wrong. God has forgiven our lengthy debt to Him so we must always forgive any size debt that others have with us. No debt anybody else has with us can even compare to the debt we once had with God!

"But if we confess our sins to Him, He is faithful and just to forgive us and cleanse us from every wrong."

~1 John 1:9

It is important for us to live a life of repentance while constantly giving our sins to God so we can not only be forgiven, but cleansed as well. As we remain clean, forgive others, and believe; we are able to operate more in the "supernatural" than if we were guilty, shameful, bitter, and unfaithful. This is all very important when it comes to our prayers for others to become healed!

We want to be as useful as possible for God's Kingdom. Shame will bring defeat to any ministry. We are over-comers and over-comers must not be defeated! We will triumph over our obstacles and overcome our failures continuously through the power of Christ. Sicknesses and evil are simply consequences for the fallen world we live in. However, Jesus is the solution to such problems!

"That evening many demon-possessed people were brought to Jesus. He cast out the evil spirits with a simple command, and He *healed* all the sick."

~ Matthew 8:16

This exemplifies Jesus' kind nature. And if you remember right, the Spirit of Christ (Holy Spirit) produces a fruit with 9 different departments that all make up the same fruit. Joy, peace, love, faithfulness, gentleness, kindness, goodness, self-control, and patience are what all make up this fruit. So, it is very much like Jesus' nature to *heal* people.

The Holy Spirit rests on believers of today's world which gives us all supernatural capabilities and the desire to *heal* people just like Jesus did. Let me make one thing clear, though. It is never a man that heals another man. It is the Spirit of Christ that heals everyone and anyone. Clay can't fix clay. It is the clay maker that fixes the clay. It is the blood of Jesus that purifies the man.

Back in the day, when there were clay makers and shepherds tending the sheep of the fields before Christ had been born... the clay makers and the shepherds worked together quite often. You see, the clay maker would regularly have clients who he made pots for come by and bring him a clay pot or two to fix. The clay pots may have been damaged with either cracks or sometimes even complete breaks. So, when a client would bring this clay maker a pot the maker would inspect the pot and figure out a way to fix it. Once the clay maker had decided the break would be no problem to fix he would tell his client to come back in a day or two and it would be fixed "better than before." So, the clay maker would add some wet mud to the pot and let it dry. he needed to throw it in the furnace to be complete, but before he could do that he had to do one more thing. He would take a leather bag with him to a shepherd and ask the shepherd if he could take all the tics off some of the shepherds sheep. The shepherd would usually allow that. So, this clay maker would collect numerous tics and place them in this leather bag. When he got home he would smash the leather bag with all the tics in it and out came "the blood of the lamb."

This blood would be smeared in the cracks and all around the clay pot before being thrown into the furnace. Then, the clay maker would wait and listen to the pot as it would make screaming sounds. He would wait and wait until he heard the pot make a beautiful singing type sound as it stood in the fire. He would then take it out and the clay pot would be in better shape than it ever was before. He would then hand it over to his client. His client would then inspect it and wonder how in the world this clay pot got in such great shape. The answer is, because of the "blood of the Lamb." You see, Jesus and what He did for us is what causes the supernatural to be present among us all as we are living on this earth today. The clay maker could not have fixed this clay pot if it hadn't been for the "blood of the lamb."

He was able to use it and when he used it, it made a large difference, but without it there wouldn't have been a chance! Without Jesus in my life today, my prayers would not be as powerful as they are and my speech would be useless. It is the Spirit of Christ that enables the supernatural here on this planet today.

Teaching, preaching, and healing are the 3 main aspects of ministry. These were the 3 components of Jesus' ministry. We must learn from Jesus and concentrate on what He did so we can follow Him closer. The closer we follow behind Jesus the more powerful we become in performing within the supernatural.

"Jesus traveled throughout the region of Galilee, teaching in the synagogues and announcing the Good News about the Kingdom. And He *healed* every kind of disease and illness."

~ Matthew 4:23

His concern for our wholeness has been signified by His healing. He is concerned for our understanding which is why He has called many to teach the Gospel. He preached Himself because of His concern for our commitment. Healing is what Jesus Christ did and by Him leaving this planet after being Resurrected from the dead, He left us with the Holy Spirit who gives us the very same power He has. How beautiful it is to know and love Jesus Christ as Savior. Thank God for the Holy Spirit and such power to operate within supernatural potential.

Jesus has given us dominion over sickness and death by replacing our old spirit with a counselor such as the Holy Spirit.

"Then He sent them out to tell everyone about the Kingdom of God and to *heal* the sick."

~ Luke 9:2

Notice that Jesus sent His disciples out to preach, teach, and heal. How committed are you? How much do you desire for others to understand?

You must first understand enough for yourself to experience the joy and rush it is to then share with others everything you have learned so that they will also understand. For you to be a believer today, that also means you are one of Jesus' disciples. Now answer to the Great Commission by "Going to make disciples of many nations by teaching them what Jesus has taught you." It is important to be baptized with water to simply represent the family you choose to be a part of and the God you choose to serve.

The Father, The Son, and The Holy Spirit complete God with sovereignty. Do you believe in *healing* at this point? If not stretch out your faith like you would your hamstring. Push it to its limits. Don't ask how. Don't ask why. Focus on Jesus and meditate on sovereignty, supernatural power, the deposits He has made, the withdrawals available for you, and the wonderful healing power of an amazing God!

"ALL OF MY RELATIONSHIPS IN LIFE ARE CENTERED AROUND ONE RELATIONSHIP AND THAT IS MY RELATIONSHIP WITH JESUS CHRIST. THE RELATIONSHIP I HAVE WITH CHRIST LEADS ME INTO PROSPERITY WITH ALL OF MY OTHER RELATIONSHIPS."

~ TY FORD

Chapter 14: Endurance

Patience is an earned gift! To be able to endure all things requires "patience."

When I think of endurance my mind drifts back to my football playing days. High school trained me to have a high endurance because of all the running and strength training. I got up to where I could jog 5 miles like it was nothing! Running sprints over and over again required both patience and endurance. Patience and endurance both go hand in hand.

The Bible talks about "patient endurance" in 2 Peter 1 where it talks about the Divinity of Jesus. To have faith produces a life of moral excellence. How can my morals have their proper boundaries without there being a desire for moral boundaries? In other words, without believing in God and having faith in Him there would be no desire for me to set up moral boundaries. For example, when I did not care for God I did drugs, sold drugs, and robbed other drug dealers. That is a prime example of poor moral boundaries. In other words, I was far from "moral excellence" because I did not have any faith in God. I knew there was a God but did not care to know Him enough for my faith to be placed in Him. Then you go from moral excellence to knowing God to self-control to "patient endurance" to godliness. From godliness you are able to have brotherly kindness or "philein" love. And from brotherly kindness we are able to attain charity or "agape" love.

Agape love is a godly kind of love. "Philein" love is having love for your Christian brothers and sisters. Charity or "agape" love is when you can seriously have "genuine" love for everyone including believers and non-believers.

Jesus teaches us to hate the sin and not the sinner. Think about it, Jesus came into this world to set all us sinners free. Read John 3:16. But, then read John 3:17. Verse 16 delivers us from hell and grants us eternal life in Heaven. Verse 17 tells us that God did not send His Son, Jesus to this world to **condemn** it but so that through Him we may be **saved**.

Jesus came to conquer death so that we may put our faith and trust in Him so we can be set free from sin and conquer death just like He did so we can go be with Him forever and ever! Jesus came down to this earth and served us. He did not come down here, live in a mansion, and demand us to serve Him. He showed us what it is to serve God. Jesus served the Father the entire time He lived. He was obedient to the Father for the benefit and sake of the entire Kingdom of God. What we do for the Kingdom of God benefits all who surround us! Jesus is our example. He is the portrait we are to do our best to mimic when we look in the mirror. What are we doing in life and how well are we following Him?

In order to follow Christ for the remainder of our lives, we must have the "endurance" that it takes. First we must have faith. Then we must line ourselves up with His will and His teachings so that our moral boundaries line up with His excellence. Once we line ourselves up with His will we will most definitely know Him much better than before. Once we get to know Him, that relationship grows. You spend time with your spouse day after day and your relationship grows. Same goes for a relationship with Jesus Christ.

All of my relationships in life are centered around one relationship and that is my relationship with Jesus Christ. The relationship I have with Christ leads me into prosperity with all of my other relationships. He pours so much into me that it overflows from me into those other people. Me getting to know God comes by time spent with Him and the more time I spend with Him the better I am able to do at getting to know others from the inside out. It is the inner beauty that illuminates a person from inside out. The more beauty you recognize from within a person, the more beautiful that person will become as a whole. Once we know God we are able to have better self-control. How is that? Well, the more I know God the more I am able to trust Him. The more I trust Him the more I rely on His strength instead of my own to have the self-control I desire. Knowing God makes us want to have self-control. "Patient-endurance" is once again an earned gift. Look at where we started. We started with faith and went from there all the way to patient endurance. How many steps was that?

3 steps in-between faith and "patient-endurance." How hard was it for me to simply have faith alone? Pretty hard!

The next three steps were just as hard, but it all started with faith. I can't stress enough how "patient-endurance" is truly an earned gift. But, wow! How much of an appreciated gift it is! It is a battle to keep what we have earned too!

"Patient-endurance" is what leads into love of both "philein" and "agape" styles. Without both patience and endurance I am unable to love others the way I need to love them.

How I love people is so crucial. I spent most all my life loving the "eros" kind of way. Eros is an erotic kind of love or sexual kind of love. I used to only see woman as a sex item. I had to grow up! Women are useful for far more than sex. They are nurturing, loving, and strong characters. They have been made by God to love children that may not even love them. They have been made by God to put up with us men who have abandoned them and treated them poorly out of either our poor decisions or also our anger that outrages. My mother always loved me even when I was verbally abusive to her. I am ashamed to even admit that, but in my drug addiction I was an angry person and I was mean to my own mother. But, she still loved me. She always forgave me. And, she hasn't even brought any of that up since. Women are so nice to have for moral support. They are loving creatures in a very forgiving, tender, and compassionate kind of way.

A godly woman is one to cherish forever and give God praise for. A godly woman will always have your back! She will believe in you when you don't even believe in yourself!

After writing the rough draft of this book I got married. It was December 12, 2015 I married my best friend, Hillary Ford. When I wrote the rough draft of this book I hadn't even met her yet. But, in between my rough draft and final copy of this book we got married and began doing ministry together while also growing a family.

We got married and began growing the family quickly. When we married, I became the father of two children of hers she brought in. A son who was four when we married and a daughter who was eight at that time. The daughter lives with Hillary's grandmother and the son lives with us. He calls me dad and I call him my son.

Hillary got pregnant the first month of marriage and gave birth to our son Tyler on September 29th, 2016. By the time he was born I felt so blessed to have only been married a year and already have three children. Not only that but I found somewhere I had written down that two years from then I would be living in a beautiful home with a beautiful family and come to find out that's exactly what happened. Praise God!

What is endurance? "Maintaining commitment to a goal during times of pressure. Knowing when and how to invest your time and energy. Keeping your focus on the objective God has given you. And, recognizing and laying aside all hindrances." When you make a commitment how often have you decided to give up or quit? Don't do that. That's the very opposite of "endurance." You must persevere and never give up. Be relentless!

Be like a William Wallace type warrior on the battlefield like in the movie Braveheart! There will most definitely be times of pressure in any kind of commitment that you ever decide to make. Marriage, job, children, etc. We all have many commitments all going on at once.

We don't want to give up on any of them. We don't want to be in a Fantasy Football league that causes us to be checked out in our relationships with others. I know a guy that knows a guy like that. That would hinder us into how we invest our time and energy. Is Fantasy Football league really worth all that time and energy? You figure how much time and energy it takes. Constant paying attention to football so much to where you are not only watching your favorite team and games that are on but you are even checking all kinds of other games too! I am not saying don't have a hobby that you enjoy but let's see what is more important to invest time and energy in. If I am more invested in someone I don't know that plays football on TV like Adrian Peterson than my own kids, then I may need to reevaluate some things in my life. A man's failure is because of his very own broken focus. What is breaking your focus?

It may be Fantasy Football or it may be idle time that you enjoy literally doing nothing. So what are some hindrances in our lives we must recognize? When we figure them out, we must lay them aside.

"And let us not get tired of doing what is right for after a while we will reap a harvest of blessings IF we do NOT get discouraged and give up."

~ Galatians 6:9

Keep on keeping on, and as we keep it up we will reap that harvest beyond what we could ever see when we first got started. The wonderful thing about investing time in God and doing stuff for Him is we will see a much better harvest later than we ever imagined. Also, keep in mind that you do not get so busy doing stuff for God that you miss out on living from God. The more time we spend with God, the more empowered we become to live from Him.

When I go to preach the Word of God, I want to preach it in such a way that it's as if I just came from Him. Be mindful of this, the harvest is always more plentiful than we ever imagined it would be. It may not be a bigger harvest always in quantity but in quality it surely will be. We can't give up or we will never see it!

To get discouraged is to raise a red flag for you because once you are discouraged you are on the verge of giving up. But the thing about that is you can jump into "power up" mode and recognize your back is against the wall and you got to push through. Don't miss the blessings!

They are always good and always plentiful. Nothing in life that is easy to come by is worth having.

"Wealth from get rich quick schemes quickly disappear but wealth from hard work grows."

~ Proverbs 13:11

I sold drugs and made an absolute killing! It seems I could have possibly made somewhere near a million dollars before I even turned 25 years old. Not sure how much exactly, but it was a lot. However, I had nothing to show for it other than a pair of boots. I can't believe I still have the boots! They are some nice elephant boots and I sure will tell you that if those boots could talk, boy they would tell you some stories!

So all that wealth from those get rich quick schemes most definitely disappeared quickly. However, since the day of my salvation until now I have worked hard. My hard work has been labor before The Lord to see His Kingdom increase and be edified. The wealth I am a part of today has grown from my consistency and The Lord's faithfulness.

I have a beautiful 3 bedroom house that's all brick. I have plenty of vehicles for my family and the ministries. I have a wife and 3 beautiful children. I have friends and mentors that stick by me through thick and thin.

Fourth Day Ministries has been given houses and property for Kingdom building and people building. I am no longer chasing the wind of satisfaction. I am now catching the dream of fulfillment. Fulfillment and blessings are a reality for me today. Wealth from get-rich-quick schemes will quickly disappear. However, wealth from hard work grows.

The Word of God is solid truth! It amazes me how true it all is. You reap what you sow. Wealth grows from hard work. Praying for things with the belief that you have received and actually receiving. I was just a young outlaw that gave this stuff a shot and now it kind of cracks me up how young I am and how much I have prospered just from reading truth and living to apply it. All I did was literally give it a shot.

"Pay close attention to what you hear. The closer you listen- the more understanding you will be given, and you will receive even more!"

~ Mark 4:24

That is so true too!

"If any man be in Christ, he is a new creature. Old things have gone and passed away. Behold, all things are become new."

~2 Corinthians 5:17

I believed in Christ and have been totally made new. All that old mess I did has surely passed away. Things sure have become new!

"And do not be conformed to this world, but be transformed by the renewing of your mind, that you may prove what is that good and acceptable and perfect will of God."

~ Romans 12:2 (NKJV)

Sovereignty of Christ

My mind has surely been renewed. The renewal of my mind has led me to this transformation that I am living within today. This transformation has caused me to live a life in the perfect will of God.

In the perfect will of God I have lined myself up to receive the blessings He has promised to those who love Him and walk according to His ways. My obedience to The Lord is inspired by my love for Him. His love for me inspired into me a desire to obey Him day in and day out!

2 Chronicles 7:14 talks about those that pray, seek God's face, turn away from wicked ways, and humble themselves will be forgiven and their land will be healed. The healing of the land pertains to everything in a person's life becoming healed. If a farm's land were to be healed the crops would be producing a pretty nice yield. People in my life have been saved that I never thought would ever even seek after such a thing. People who were broken in my life are now on fire for God.

People who didn't stand a chance in this world are now assets to this country. Relationships in my life that were scarred severely are now prospering. Not to mention Romans 10:9,10 talks about confessing Jesus is Lord and believing in Him in order to be saved.

This journey began with me accepting Christ in such a way. It is obvious that such salvation was granted because if it had not been I would still be getting high destroying homes by selling drugs.

"Dear brothers and sisters, whenever trouble comes your way let it be an opportunity for joy. For when your faith is tested, your endurance has a chance to grow. So let it grow, for when your endurance becomes fully developed you will be strong in character and ready for anything."

~ James 1:2-4

So, be joyful in trials? Why? We are shaped up by them is why. How we handle them develops our character. The type of character we have tells us the kind of person we are. Others also can tell who a person is by their character. Faith is the rock that sharpens patience and patience is the rock that sharpens faith. They go hand in hand. So when our faith is tested, it is our patience or our endurance that propels us through that test. And once we power through trials by our endurance, our character becomes better refined for it. So yes, be joyful during such opportunities. It is in our hardest trials where we learn obedience.

You may be reading this saying to yourself, "Whoever wrote this is absolutely nuts!" And yes you are pretty much correct in your observation. I am pretty nuts. However, the passage came from words inspired by God and written by man. God is pretty nuts Himself. He died for us. Heaven went bankrupt for you and me. God sent His best. He sent His only Son so that you and I could be saved through Him. He has invested His best into us. It's important that we steward Him well by obeying Him. Who cares that much about anyone to actually die for them when they don't have to? God does! The Father, Son, and Holy Spirit all hold up a pretty amazing level of sovereignty.

The Holy Spirit has had me say some pretty crazy things before and continues to uphold that streak. The Father is pretty bold to have created us interesting characters and to also have sent His beloved Son in this world to die for us. But, do these words not uphold an extreme truth? I know that if they slap me across the face then they must also do the same for you too.

"Not only that, but we rejoice in our sufferings, knowing that suffering produces endurance, and endurance produces character, and character produces hope, and hope does not put us to shame, because God's love has been poured into our hearts through the Holy Spirit who has been given to us."

~ Romans 5:3-5

So, suffering produces endurance and endurance produces character. Then, character produces hope and hope puts us not to shame. Where we find hope, there is love that sustains that hope. This basically says the same thing that James 1:2-4 tells us except just in a different way. This is what I would call a "cross-reference." A cross reference is where two Scriptures basically support one another and say close to the same thing and support one another as truth.

"Even though Jesus was God's Son, He learned obedience from the things He suffered."

~ Hebrews 5:8

Therefore, if Christ learned obedience by what He suffered, we must also take advantage of our suffering and let it produce obedience in us. It is through suffering we learn to obey The Lord. It is through testing that we cling to God and lean on His teachings to help empower us for obedience.

"For you have been given not only the privilege of trusting in Christ, but also the privilege of suffering for Him."

~ Philippians 1:29

It is a privilege to suffer for Christ because it gives us the opportunity to learn obedience. Obedience is what God blesses. He can't bless disobedience! God can turn everything around for the good in our lives once we learn to obey Him. Love and obedience are synonymous.

"And we know that God causes everything to work together for the good of those who love God and are called according to His purpose for them."

~ Romans 8:28

In other words, it doesn't matter how much damage we did. What matters is that once we decide to obey God because we love Him, He will turn it all around for the good!

I hope that by reading this chapter you recognize the importance of patience and endurance or "patient-endurance," and I hope that you now know what it takes to earn it and are able to envision the rewards for having it. May today find you well as you push through whatever tests you. What matters is that in the end your character is refined, causing you to be a stronger asset for God's Kingdom and a better person in today's world.

"REPENTANCE IS THE ONE THING GOD CALLED US TO MODEL THAT HE COULDN'T MODEL HIMSELF."

~TY FORD

CHAPTER 15:
Value of Self-Control

Wow! This chapter is for me more than anyone else. Self-control, just like patience, is also an earned gift. Patience is a rock that sharpens our self-control. Being patient requires self-control and vice versa.

If I am waiting in a drive thru line and honking the horn because of how slow the line is moving, my self-control has slipped up because of my impatience. It takes a little self-control to endure patience just like it takes a little patience to enable self-control. I used to be that guy that honked my horn in drive-thrus, flashed my bright lights behind people on the interstate, and flipping the bird to people anywhere I felt necessary. I had ZERO self-control and ZERO patience. I had endurance but that was because I had NO choice! I used to go nuts waiting on my drug dealer in Memphis to turn into an apartment complex where I was waiting for him. I would anticipate every next car was going to be his. I stayed looking for that white Monte Carlo! I didn't have the self-control to sit there, chill, and let him pull up without me jerking my neck every next car that pulled in. However, I had no choice but to endure my lack of patience, my lack of self-control, and the torment it all caused me. Obviously, you would expect for me to have a lot more self-control now than I did then. It has gotten a lot better. However, I still have some major mountains to climb and that's alright because guess who is going to be helping me climb them? That's right, Jesus Christ!

My best friend is my God. I serve a great God! He is with me during all my times of frustrations that are caused by my lack of self-control. He teaches me to have self-control by His own control taking charge of the circumstances around me. For example, I may be checking my phone for someone to respond back to something I said or answer something I have asked them. I used to be a drug dealer which has led me into outstanding phone etiquette skills today, but has also caused me to expect everyone else to have the same punctuality with communication on their end. That is because of my poor self-control. I am beginning to grasp patience and endurance. However, my self-control is a little bit harder to earn. Thankfully, I am a step ahead because of what patience I have already earned. Endurance is the stepping stone to patience and patience is the ladder to self-control.

I will tell you that my self-control has gotten to be great with biting my lip to avoid saying things I don't have any business saying. I have gotten cussed out a lot on this new journey. You may be thinking, "How are you getting cussed out by church people?" Well, if I am a doctor working in the emergency room then how in the world would I not get some blood on me? Church is a hospital for sinners. Yes, the church is full of hypocrites! Shoot, I am one myself to a certain "extent." I know what's right and wrong and know how to teach it all but that does not mean I always do right!

My righteousness is a gift from God. I can't depend on my own righteousness because that would come by obedience to Mosaic law and guess what? I am surely bound to break one of them and every time I do it is as if I broke them all. The Word says, "Our own righteousness is as equivalent to that of a menstrual rag." Good Lord!

We obviously need God. Thank God that justice from that righteousness does not serve me. Furthermore, thank God that because of Grace I am the righteousness of God in Christ Jesus (2 Corinthians 5:21).

Thank God I don't get what I deserve by justice, but I get what I don't deserve by faith in Jesus Christ and my acceptance for what He did for me at the Cross. By justice I would get what I deserve, but by Grace I get what I don't deserve which is far better than I could ever deserve!

"All have sinned and fall short of the glory of God being justified as a gift by His Grace through the redemption which is in Christ Jesus."

~Romans 3:23,24

May I raise my hand and tell you that I fall short!? Because, I sure do! However, I am not about to let my shortcomings interfere with my work in helping save people's lives for eternity. Not happening Jack! People are still imperfect in church but once they have gotten into a deep relationship with their Creator by going to that church over and over again, guess what? They are not as imperfect as they used to be!

People go to the gym because they are all out of shape to a "certain extent," but you don't stop going because of them do you? Well, don't be run off from church because of the "people."

Go to church because you want more of God! I go to the gym for the same reason everyone else goes, which is to get in a little better shape than I was when I first started going! Back to self-control... This all really applies to self-control and you could even say, "discipline." To have self-control is to be "disciplined." I discipline myself to go to church. I discipline myself to read the Word of God. I discipline myself to listen to Christian music the majority of the time. I am listening to Newsboys Restart CD at this very moment. That's not the only kind of music I listen to. I listen to everything, Christian genre or secular genre. I am not concerned as much about whether or not the music is secular or not. I'm concerned with the message of the music. If it's vulgar and worldly I don't want any part in it. Why? Because I must guard my soul gates. When you take garbage in, it deposits garbage into your heart, which is bound to come out later. Nobody should want that.

I must be careful what all I listen to or watch because if I hear and see vulgarity, my thinking could very well be altered and heart affected negatively. I discipline myself to listen to preaching on CD's. I discipline myself to write this book with all the diligence and devotion it requires! I discipline myself to train daily.

You may say, "Train daily?" ..."What do you mean?" ...I mean that if I am to teach, preach, write, and speak about Jesus I must grow in the knowledge I have of Who He is.

"Do you not know that in a race all the runners run, but only one receives the prize? So run that you may obtain it. Every athlete exercises self- control in all things. They do it to receive a perishable wreath, but we an imperishable. So I do not run aimlessly; I do not box as one beating the air. But I discipline my body and keep it under control, lest after preaching to others I myself should be disqualified."

~1 Corinthians 9:24-27

You see, I am on the same page as Paul. I train myself to not do things not because I can't handle the consequences for my own personal journey, but so that I don't cause anyone to stumble. I want to live as godly a life possible because all eyes are on those who teach and preach the Truth. I don't get high anymore because that would disqualify me from taking part in Kingdom works. I am not a servant of God because I am so good. It is because He is so good, and it is truly an honor to be a part of something so big. I thought it was cool to get paychecks from the PGA Tour when I worked at Southwind Tournament Players Club in Memphis, Tennessee. But, it is way neater to receive blessings from God and His Kingdom. Just knowing Who I work for is rewarding enough in itself. So, yes it may be hard to train myself to not check my phone or check my Facebook so much but I have learned the importance of self-control from a Kingdom perspective. Without proper self-control I would be unable to minister to those in need.

I learned how important it is to just listen. If I don't care to hear what anyone else has to say, how can I expect them to listen to what I have to say? Yes, I may have the solution in my response. But, how can I present the solution the way they need to hear it if I have not listened to them thoroughly? What I hear them say as I listen often leads me in how I say what I have to say. As a Minister, I must establish common ground before presenting the solution. The solution is always Christ indefinitely, but the person needs to have Christ presented to them within their own reach. That is why listening is so important. A good conversationalist is what?... A good "listener."

"So think clearly and exercise self-control. Look forward to the gracious salvation that will come to you when Jesus Christ is revealed to the whole world."

~ 1 Peter 1:13

A sound mind helps us think with much more clarity. Such clarity enlightens our perception, which then enhances our reality. The way we see things can be traced back to the good ole cup analogy that is either "half full or half empty." What are you grateful for? Do you see the problems or do you search for the solutions? Just for today I search for the solutions! I plan on doing the same thing tomorrow too! For every problem there is a solution and His name is Jesus! Jesus is the answer to everything. You may be thinking, "But my knee hurts so bad and I have prayed and prayed for it to heal but it hasn't!" In those situations, we must put our *trust* completely in Him. As Isaiah 55:8,9 tells us His ways are higher than ours just as His thoughts are as well, we must trust in His higher ways and higher thoughts. He is always working for our benefit. Your injured knee may be holding you back from doing something that could really hurt you. Even when we lose a family member, He is totally looking out because that family member is going home and we are able to experience all that love that person caused us to feel over a lifetime!

Grief and sorrow helps me understand the sentimental value of love. I had to lose a few friends before I could learn to appreciate a good friend for what they are truly worth. God is always in control and He is always looking out! Trust in God. He will never let you down! Let your trust be "without" borders! Having a sound mind helps us acknowledge the importance of exhibiting self-control.

Self-control is worth having for our own salvation alone. But, for the salvation of others??

Are we willing to exercise a little more self-control so that other lives may be changed, saved, and transformed? I am totally on board! Who is with me!? What do we have to lose anyways?

We have everything to gain! Lives being changed and families being restored! It takes obedience to have the self-control we wish to attain. Once we attain self-control we must exercise it daily to sustain it.

Proverbs is such a great book. It is the "wisdom" book of the Old Testament. James is the "wisdom" book of the New Testament. There are often controversies over the Old Testament and New Testament. Some choose one side over the other and that is rather foolish. We have been given the entire book for a reason. The Old Testament goes hand in hand with the New and vice versa. We would not understand holiness without the Old Testament and we would not understand salvation without the New Testament. Holiness and salvation are both important. Grace is also very important and I see grace in both Testaments.

"For The Lord sees clearly what a man does, examining every path he takes. An evil man is held captive by his own sins; they are ropes that catch and hold him. He will die for lack of *self-control*; he will be lost because of his great foolishness."

~ Proverbs 5:21-23

The Lord does see what we always do and there are consequences He has implemented into this universe to help us respect His boundaries of righteousness and wickedness. When we live righteously, we will reap the good consequences. If we live out of wickedness and evil, we will reap bad consequences. It is because of grace that we still reap blessings we don't deserve though. Our own sins are like ropes that catch us and hold us back from blessings God has in store for us. God wants to bless us. Where there is obedience in one's life, blessings will be found.

Sometimes we disqualify ourselves from certain blessings. I believe that no matter what I do I will still be a blessed man because God is just that good. However, I view Him as the quarterback calling the huddle while I am the receiver. He tells me what route to run and how to run it so I can catch the pass in the end zone and score a touchdown to win the game. If I don't run the route He has **instructed** me to run then I won't reap the good consequences a touchdown reception will offer me. I won't be getting high fives from everyone and chants from the crowd. My team would have lost and I would have felt ashamed for running the route poorly. God's Word is full of instructions on how to live to get in line to receive His abundant blessings.

We get in line with His will, we receive abundant blessing, and we are offered the protection that comes with being in His will. The skull protects the brain. The brain functions properly inside the skull and is protected by being inside the skull. However, if you take the brain outside the skull it won't function at all and it would have then surrendered all protection that the skull had to offer. By being in God's will we are in line to receive His promises with a hedge of protection around us. A little self-control is worth all of that!

God's will offers provision, protection and peace. Just like the brain has that inside of the skull, we also have that inside of God's will.

Another great passage from Proverbs is Proverbs 16:32 where Solomon says, "Better to be patient than powerful; better to have **self-control** than to conquer a city."

Conquering a city is powerful. But, it says that to be patient is "better" than to be powerful. Patience overrides power here in this Scripture. A city has a lot going on in it and usually holds large value.

Sovereignty of Christ

Conquering a city is powerful because you are conquering something that holds a lot of value. But, self-control and patience put to shame the power of conquering a city. With self-control and patience we can conquer the world. That is what God had Solomon say in this passage. Does that tell you something? If I exhibit self-control and patience while talking to everyone I talk to in a day then guess what? Everyone I talked to recognized the patience and self-control whether it was consciously or subconsciously.

"As iron sharpens iron, a friend sharpens a friend."

~ Proverbs 27:17

Don't you realize, we all rub off on one another. So, if patience and self-control rubs off on 12 people I talk to and 12 more people that they talk to and etc, etc...

We have begun conquering the world! So, shall we begin conquering today!? Let's do this!

"Older men are to be sober- minded, dignified, self- controlled, sound in faith, in love, and in steadfastness."

~ Titus 2:2

By older men being sober-minded, dignified, self-controlled, sound in faith, in love, and in steadfastness; they are passing these qualities down to the younger generations. The youth of today look up to the older generation, or used to at least! It is supposed to be that way. Has the younger generation felt condemned for some reason?

"God sent His Son into the world not to judge (condemn) the world, but to *save* the world through Him."

~ John 3:17

So if God sent His Son to save the world and not to judge or condemn us then many ought to run to Jesus. He is so good! God will judge the world eventually but not until so many people are saved first. Jesus tells us in John 13:34,35; "**A new commandment I give to you, that you love one another: just as I have loved you, you also are to love one another. By this all people will know that you are my disciples, if you have love for one another.**"

Therefore, if we are to change the world we must show people Jesus. Only way we can do that is to love each other the way He has loved us. How has He loved us? With compassion and not condemnation. We can't love people with condemnation because there is no such thing. We must love people with that "agape" style to it.

The godly love is what we are talking about here! When we do that, people will take notice, and disciples will be made; causing the world to be changed. Let's exercise some patience and self-control today so we can get started with this mission: *To Change The World!*

"GRIEF AND SORROW HELPS ME UNDERSTAND THE SENTIMENTAL VALUE OF LOVE. I HAD TO LOSE A FEW FRIENDS BEFORE I COULD LEARN TO APPRECIATE A GOOD FRIEND FOR WHAT THEY ARE TRULY WORTH."

~TY FORD

CHAPTER 16:
Lust vs Love

I am not all that excited to write a chapter on every man's weakness because I am a man and this chapter has most definitely been one of my biggest weaknesses before I got married. However, this is probably one of the most important chapters for any man or woman to read.

We live in a world where sex is okay and accepted in various cultures. A young boy growing up is told to have become grown once he "gets laid." It is wrong for our world to recognize boys as a young man once they have lost their virginity but to look down on the girls for the same thing. I have a problem with that. If teenagers were looked at the same way between both genders once that took place in their lives I would not have as big of a problem with it, but it would still be an issue. Men are often seen as "victorious" for the notches they earn under their belt while the women are put to "shame" for their devious acts. There is glory in virginity. The younger generation needs encouragement to guard their virginity until marriage.

Lust can be referred to as "eros" type love. "Eros" basically stands for erotic love. You think about the word erotic and you probably think of Adam Sandler in the movie, Billy Madison, where he is so excited on "nudie magazine" day! He runs around all day exclaiming, "nudie magazine day, nudie magazine day, nudie magazine day!" Poor Billy loved his posing women. A lot of men are literally like that whether it be with magazines, videos, or actual women.

Why?

Well, that's the norm of society. I grew up with an eagerness to have sex and after my experiences of it, the eagerness was a part of my daily routine. Sex got in the way of God's love.

"Agape" love is godly kind of love. It is impossible to love someone "agape" style with sex being part of that relationship and out of God's will. Sex was made by God, but designed for marriage. It's perverted if not done in His will. There's no point in hiding any of my mistakes as I write this chapter because my mistakes have caused me to grow in understanding. It is important to understand the reasoning behind sex being designed for marriage only.

There's no glory in sex before marriage. In fact, it creates ungodly soul ties that hinder both participating parties all the way until those soul ties are broken by the power in Christ. Hearing about sex being only designed for marriage after the life I had lived did not make a lick of sense! Hearing the truth wasn't enough for me, so I ventured my way down to lustful lane once again thinking nothing of it. But, the conviction that came afterward was pretty awful. There was not any enjoyment to such an act. I was disobedient and my disobedience reaped it's consequences. Those consequences were not good. The devil sought after me viciously with his condemnation. Fortunately, the knowledge of Romans 8:1 provided comfort in the growth from such failure; **"So now there is therefore no condemnation for those who belong to Christ Jesus."**

The Holy Spirit does not participate in sin that we are ever involved in. What does that mean?

Well, the Holy Spirit provides comfort and love. Without that comfort and love, how is something that is supposed to feel good going to really feel good at all? It clearly won't feel as good as it even did before we were exposed to the truth. But, once there is marriage and sex is carried out in an "agape" fashion with the Holy Spirit involved, then there comes the extra comfort and love that becomes involved with both parties!

Many people want to secretly have sex with others but do all they can to avoid talking about it. Why not talk about it? It is so prevalent in today's society. Shouldn't it be an issue to talk about? Maybe it's that many people know deep down that they are doing it out of God's will so they try to cover it up and hide it to avoid the shame and guilt. God is not condemning but the Holy Spirit is Who convicts us. The devil will whisper lies in our ears causing us to feel shame, condemnation, and guilt. But, he is a liar who comes to steal, kill, and destroy. But, Jesus has come into our lives to give us life in ABUNDANCE! God wants us to have an awesome life full of **blessings**! He gives us His Word so that we can hear His word and follow it's instructions. This gives us the opportunity to get in line to receive His promises.

If you're having sex out of God's will, I encourage you to make it right by either staying away from whoever you need to stay away from, or getting married. God is like a star quarterback for the home team. We are His receivers. We run the route He tells us to run so we can maybe catch the game winning touchdown pass. Every day has its new routes. They are all given to us by the same Word though. The Word is like a gigantic playbook!

What route is He telling you to run today?

Run that route His Way and you will be blessed for it! Consider the reward a surprise, but beneficial. Therefore, find someone that means a lot to you. Find someone you are willing to have a relationship with God's way. God is the glue to relationships! Sometimes, it's really not worth having sex with someone and risking the destruction of that relationship. Someone worth having is worth the patience and self-control it takes to allow the relationship to develop in something that lasts forever.

We all make mistakes, especially in this arena! Like I have said, I have made mistakes before I got saved and even after. It took me making the mistake a couple of times before I could grasp an understanding on the importance of abstinence until marriage. Before getting married, I had experienced relationships in "eros'" fashion and have come to realize that "agape" is the way. I married the love of my life and we waited until after we were married to have sex.

God has blessed us for that! Sex only lasts so long. Doesn't matter who you are! The intimacy of talking and spending time with one another outlasts sex for all age groups regardless of the circumstances. Therefore, the intimacy that lasts the longest is obviously what is most important.

My whole life has changed now that I don't focus living life with the agendas I had in the past. Loving people from the inside out and recognizing their inner beauty affects their outward appearance. The way you treat someone can cause them to glow. Today, I am happily married and the way I treat my wife is very capable of giving her a glow. I don't love my wife as a sex item. I love my wife as a co-heir and help mate. She completes me as God makes us both whole.

Some of you may read this and get online searching for a bride or groom! Be careful with that. That is more dangerous than having sex with someone recreationally. You rush off to Las Vegas and marry a stripper that leads to a wonderful evening and a miserable life that follows. You married a person to get laid and now you are stuck with them until you figure out a way to make it work or get a divorce. Either way, that will sure leave a scar.

My suggestion considering marriage is to allow a relationship to develop with God in the center for at least a year before even considering any kind of life-long commitment. It may seem like an awfully tough obstacle. Ask any old married couple about their marriage and they will be the first to tell you it sure ain't easy! The development over a year or however much longer lays the foundation for there to be a healthy marriage built upon.

To rush a relationship into marriage just for sex is just as much "living in the flesh" as sleeping around with everyone at the local "hole in the wall" bar. However, I will say that my wife and I got married after only knowing one another for a couple months. But, we heard from God and that's all that mattered. However, neither one of us encourage doing that. Only if you've heard from God. We both still encourage getting to know someone for a year before marrying them. Make sure that who you are considering for marriage is extremely devoted to God. When they are devoted to God, they will be loyal to you.

In 2 Samuel 11, King David saw a beautiful woman bathing, known as Bathsheba, from the roof of his palace. So, he sent his messengers for her and they brought her back. He slept with her and got her pregnant. This woman was Uriah's wife. Uriah was a part of King David's army. David tried to set him up with her to sleep with her so the pregnancy of David's child would be covered up as his own. Uriah was so loyal to his army that he wouldn't wine and dine with his wife while they were fighting. So, King David sent this man to the front lines of war knowing it would result in his death. King David was a man after God's own heart and he murdered this man and committed adultery with his wife. He later married Bathsheba, which led to the birth of King Solomon who wrote the book of Proverbs, Song of Songs, and Ecclesiastes. David's weakness was lust. But, if David had been where he should have been in that season of his life, he wouldn't have been checking out Bathsheba like he was. David raped her.

How was it rape?

He was the King and had sent for her so she would come and have sex with him. Then he murdered Uriah. However, David repented and was restored. But, there were serious consequences he still had to face and live with. The consequences of lust are not worth the price that comes with. God causes things to work together for the good as Romans 8:28 says. We must love God enough to live a life of repentance. A life of repentance involves a lot of repenting in a world like today.

I ask God every day to search me for any wicked way so I can repent. We must not be ashamed to repent. We ought to be ashamed not to repent! Repentance is the one thing God called us to model that He couldn't model Himself. Think about it... Jesus couldn't repent because He never sinned. The Mosaic law or Ten Commandments condemns the "best" of us while the Grace of God sets free the "worst" of us. We may grow through our past failures by allowing God to work them together for the good. He has done that in my life. I used to be a drug dealer who slept around with all kinds of different women and robbed other drug dealers by force, but He has used all that to make me a minister that is able to relate with the world on a personal level. Thank God for His Grace!

In the book of John, Chapter 8, verses 1-11; Jesus helps out an adulterous woman. This adulterous woman was about to be stoned to death for her devious deeds. However, Jesus intervened by picking up a stone Himself and said, "All right, but let the one who has never sinned throw the first stone!" This scared all of those radical religious folks away. Then He asked the woman where her accusers were. Jesus told her He didn't condemn her and for her to, "Go, and sin no more." You see, Jesus sets us free and does not condemn us.

Religion is condemning but relationship with Christ is liberating. Invest in such a relationship because of its eternal value. I recommend reading the book, Song of Songs. It is a book that basically represents a dialogue of love in a sexual sense yet still under the umbrella of "agape" style. It is full of intimacy.

"Your love delights me, my treasure, my bride. Your love is better than wine, your perfume more fragrant than spices."

~ Song of Songs 4:10

That is just to give you an idea of the language used in this wonderful book of intimacy and love.

I have enjoyed writing this book. Why not totally throw myself out there for the benefit of many people? Speaking the truth reaps its rewards. I am a very blessed man today and will be even more blessed by the time tomorrow comes. May you find love inside the wonderful will of God. May your love for Him produce obedience in you that bears lasting fruit for God's Kingdom.

"MORAL EXCELLENCE AND VIRTUE OUGHT TO BE LIKE A MASS PRODUCING MACHINE WHERE INVITATIONS ARE SENT OUT FOR OTHERS TO KNOW CHRIST."

~ TY FORD

Chapter 17:
Virtue

Virtue can be described as moral excellence and goodness. Maybe you're like me and had faith at a young age that produced some excellent morals in you, but that moral excellence got set back by conforming more to the world.

"And do not be conformed to this world, but be transformed by the renewing of your mind, that you may prove what is that good and acceptable and perfect will of God."

~ Romans 12:2 (NKJV)

How do our minds become renewed? Our mind becomes renewed by reading the Word of God. Once our mind enters the stages of renewal, our perspective becomes enlightened. As our perspective becomes enlightened, our reality becomes enhanced. With an enhanced reality and an enlightened perspective, the thoughts we develop come alive with clarity.

Clarity is very valuable.

Thinking with clarity eliminates a lot of ruckus that the mind wants to produce. On the contrary, when we are conformed to the world our mind produces all that ruckus and impure mess as a result of the fear the world produces in our minds. Watch horror movies all day and recognize the results of watching such. Your mind will produce its' thoughts out of FEAR. Fear stands for False Evidence Appearing Real. Fear is perverted "faith." It works just the same as faith because it is based upon belief in something you can't fully see. Your imagination can lead you into faith or fear. Your imagination causes you to believe things.

Reflect back on your life as a kid. You believed in fairy tales. You believed in the Easter bunny, Santa Claus, the Tooth Fairy. Your imagination caused you to believe in these things. By the way, those were the days! Why can't we use that same imagination to believe in receiving the promises of God that we haven't yet seen? That would be having faith. If we exercised our faith today as adults the way we exercised them as kids we would be seriously walking by faith and living an enhanced life to the fullest! Instead, why watch the News and live our lives out of fear? Why live a life of paranoia fearing someone's waiting around every corner to mug us?

Yeah, we do live in a fallen world and maybe someday there will be someone that gets us, but with Jesus in our hearts what is there to fear about that? Are we doubting the majesty and peace there is in Heaven?

Are we scared to let go of this filthy world to step into eternity? There are going to be people we leave behind in this world that we love no matter what day God decides to call us up to be with Him. The way I see it, when God calls someone I love to be with Him in eternity I become overwhelmed with all the love I had for that person and I recognize the value of that person being in my life. So, when God calls me up to be with Him my loved ones will experience the true measure of love they had for me. Of course they would miss me just like I missed those I lost. However, Ecclesiastes tells us that there is a "time to mourn and a time to dance."

If we allowed our imaginations to carry us into the child-like faith we once had, we would literally be "standing" on the promises of God. His Word is to give us insight of such promises. For example, Mark 11:24 gives us Jesus' very own words; on this matter.

"Therefore I tell you whatever you ask in prayer, believe that you have received it, and it will be yours."

~ Mark 11:24

"Then if My people who are called by My name will humble themselves, pray, seek My face, and turn away from their wicked ways I will hear from Heaven, forgive their sins, and heal their land."

~2 Chronicles 7:14

These are instructions and directions to receiving promises. Believe and ask in Jesus name and we will receive. Pray, humble ourselves, seek God's face, and turn away from our wicked ways to have everything in our lives including house notes and relationships resolved and worked out for the good. That's what the "healing of our land" is all about.

Everything in the vicinity of our lives is becoming healed, whether it be our finances, our families being restored, or broken relationships being mended. Matthew 6:33 tells us to put God's Kingdom first and live righteously to receive everything we need. We build God's Kingdom and He will build our house and take care of our lives. That's truly how it works. Don't worry but pray about everything so you can receive the indescribable peace God waits so eagerly to give us (Philippians 4:4-8 inspired).

2 Peter 1 is all about the Divinity of Jesus or you could say, "The Divine Nature of Christ." We have faith which is our basic foundation. The faith is what produces moral excellence (or virtue). Then, the virtuous ways lead to knowing God or knowledge of who He is. That leads us into self-control, which is an earned gift just like patience. That self-control leads us into patient-endurance. Then, we are led into godliness. And, from godliness we find ourselves loving our fellow Christians which then leads us into a charity that entails genuine love for everyone.

Virtuous ways are a follow up stepping stone to our faith. The book of James talks about how faith without works is as useless as works without faith. Our best sermon should be the life we live and the heart we resemble. We must resemble a heart like Christ! Our best sermons are our actions or our works, and when necessary we may speak about it too. It is best to be about it mostly and speak about it when invited to speak about it. Righteous living spurs something in unbelievers that causes their curiosity to ask questions. That's when it is necessary to speak about it.

When we teach, speaking about Jesus and such, Good News is absolutely necessary. It would only be pointless to speak about Good News all day every day when our works resemble that of poor character. The tongue produces both venom and praises. My praises would be meaningless if the venom is coming out too! Those praises would be like the expensive perfume while the venom would be like the one stinking fly that ruined the whole batch of expensive perfume (Ecclesiastes).

Moral excellence and virtue ought to be like a mass producing machine where invitations are sent out for others to know Christ.

"As water reflects the face, so one's life ought to reflect the heart."

~ Proverbs 27:19

A heart like Christ ought to be resembled by the lives we live. I can talk about Jesus all day long to people on every street corner but if I don't personally resemble Him in my walk I am basically "spitting in the wind."

How about those times Christians get in public discussions that lead into arguments about denomination and doctrine? Is that absolutely pointless or what!? The Word of God is based upon The Trinity of all Trinities. In other words, there is a whole lot of different levels of meaning that can be brought out of each verse that is in there. It is the Living Word. What you may get out of Proverbs 27:17 could be one thing but the person next to you could get a whole other thing out of it. They may all go hand in hand but there can also be different meanings that are drawn out of the same verse.

I don't necessarily agree with any doctrine or denomination 100%. I believe that in today's world if a woman is on fire for God and doing His work she should be able to be ordained. Some denominations are against that. Women can help women better than men can just like men can help men better than women can. There is nothing wrong with a woman being ordained for a position in running a women's Next Step reentry program for Fourth Day Ministries. I can ordain whoever I want to inside my ministry, Fourth Day Ministries, and there will come a time when I will ordain a woman or maybe multiple women eventually to run different women's facilities. The first one will be my wife. Then, together we can ordain others. That may mess with some folk's religion and all I have to say about that is "Good!"

Religion has not saved anyone. Denomination has not saved anyone. However, a relationship with Jesus Christ saves everyone! My relationship with Christ has led me into prosperity. God speaks to everyone on a personal level that varies between different people.

"God works through different men in different ways but it is the same God who achieves His purposes through them all."

~ 1 Corinthians 12:6

He uses some men to represent Him in shipyards and factories while He uses others to preach in churches, preach on TV, and run ministries. Different denominations are a result of different comprehensions. Sure, maybe the devil got in the way there causing division, but when it is all said and done we are all united by one truth; that being we all worship the same God!

"In everything you do, stay away from complaining and arguing so that no one can speak a word of blame against you. You are to live clean, innocent lives as children of God in a dark world full of people who are crooked and stubborn."

~ Philippians 2:14,15

Again, if we are arguing over nonsense whether it be how old the earth really is or which doctrine is more correct, then every non believer that hears such nonsense will be pushed further away from God because they don't want to end up looking that foolish. We must be mindful that there are others always watching and we can't ever see all who are really watching. Our best sermons must be our actions and our works. Works without faith are useless because all the donations to all the charities in the world can't buy someone's ticket into Heaven. All the faith in the world without any works that resemble such faith won't help anybody else get into Heaven. Faith is a gift to be shared with others.

Proverbs 31 is all about a virtuous woman and the value that is placed on her for such virtue.

"Who can find a *virtuous* and capable wife? She is more precious than rubies. Her husband can trust her, and she will greatly enrich his life. She brings him good, not harm, all the days of her life."

~ Proverbs 31:10-12

A women who looks out for a man's well-being and best interest, will bring that man everlasting satisfaction.

A virtuous women's love doesn't have a faulty catch to it. It is pure and solid. A relationship with such a woman is built upon rock because Jesus is the center of the relationship. To speak about Jesus and to be about Jesus are two different lifestyles. When a woman who is virtuous talks about Jesus, she is very credible to whatever it is she says. But, a woman who uses Jesus as an alibi for her immoral

202

life will be counted as a fool in the long run. A virtuous woman is a woman who is full of wisdom, hardworking, strong character, lives with integrity, and filled with great compassion. A virtuous woman is virtuous because of her character and not by her looks.

A woman with great character will become attractive to any man that takes the time to notice it.

My wife is growing in The Lord and the more she grows, the more virtuous she becomes. This is so attractive to me. I love watching my wife serve God and helping her grow into who God is making her. It's amazing. She loves The Lord and is dedicated to Him. She's a virtuous woman, and I am a blessed man.

Life is not about saying the right things. It is all about standing up for what's right and helping out those who need help and are trying to help themselves. Virtue is moral excellence and goodness. How excellent are our morals and how good are we to others? Is our character where it needs to be today? If not, let's strive to get there by tomorrow!

LIFE IS NOT ABOUT SAYING THE RIGHT THINGS. IT IS ALL ABOUT STANDING UP FOR WHAT'S RIGHT AND HELPING OUT THOSE WHO NEED HELP AND ARE TRYING TO HELP THEMSELVES.

~ TY FORD

Furthermore...

It is wise to make the estimate that one's life is not made whole until that person has given their life to Christ...

The Word of God is so sovereign in the sense that it all comes together in truth. We, as human beings, embark in a lifestyle that is brought together by a purpose. We are given a specific purpose for living by our Creator.

"I am your Creator. You were in My care before you were even born."

~ Isaiah 44:2

God designed us all for a specific ministry which gives us all a purpose for living. We are called to live out that purpose. As we live out the purpose God made us for, we find fulfillment. When we are fulfilled we are constantly being filled while we are already "full." Therefore, everything we receive that is a bonus offers that much more to the people around us!

Grace is a gift and when we are being filled with grace while already full of grace, we are fortunate enough to have such a gift that we can share with others. The same concept goes for peace, joy, love, faithfulness, self-control, kindness, gentleness, goodness, and even patience. We sharpen each other like iron sharpens iron. What we exemplify rubs off on others for either their well-being or disadvantages. Goodness and wickedness are both contagious.

When we have issues in life that need to be dealt with it, is best for us to put God first and help build His Kingdom so He is given the opportunity to "heal our land." The way to handle this is to do four things, which are to pray, humble ourselves, seek God's face, and turn away from our wicked ways.

When we sow into the Kingdom we will reap from the same Kingdom we sowed into.

"Be not deceived; God is not mocked: for whatsoever a man sows, that shall he also reap. For he who sows to his flesh shall of the flesh reap corruption; but he who sows to the Spirit shall of the Spirit reap life everlasting."

~ **Galatians 6:7**

In other words, we can reap good things or bad things. When we appease the flesh we reap it's corruption. But, when we sow into the Spirit we reap spiritual blessings. Spiritual blessings give birth to physical blessings because the spiritual world gives birth to the physical world. God made light out of darkness. What makes you think He is incapable of turning your darkness into light? He will use ordinary people to do extraordinary things! I am ordinary and He is using me. He will also use you!

"Many are called but few are chosen."

~ **Matthew 22:14**

The difference between being called and being chosen is that the "chosen" always show up! When we show up we are blessed. Don't miss what God has for you. Always show up!

"For if you confess with your mouth that Jesus is Lord and believe in your heart that God raised Him from the dead you will be SAVED!"

~ **Romans 10:9**

"For God so loved the world that He gave His only Son so that everyone who believes in Him will not perish, but have eternal life."

~ **John 3:16**

Then, John 3:17 tells us that Jesus did not come into the world to condemn it, but so that through Him they might be SAVED! The devil believes in God because he has obviously been around Him face to face several times. However, the devil was unable to "accept" Jesus as THE SAVIOR. That is why the devil has the three jobs he has, which are to steal, kill, and destroy! If we only believe without having acceptance of such an awesome Savior, we are lost and confused. 99% saved is still 100% lost!

What are you doing here?

Has God given you a vision?

Have you put your vision down on paper?

Are you saved?

Then, is your salvation resulting in service to others? It ought to because that's God's heart. It is God's will that our salvation result in service to others!

Are you political in the sense of tickling others ears telling them what they want to hear? Or, are you prophetic in the sense that you are bold enough to tell people anything God leads you to tell them?

Do you love others the way God loves them? Or, do you only love people the way you feel like they deserve?

By grace we get what we don't deserve. None of us deserve salvation. It is a gift from God! It's between us and God how we steward that gift. Do you accept grace without offering it?

1 Corinthians 13 is our code for love.

"Love suffers long and is kind; love does not envy; love does not parade itself, is not puffed up; does not behave rudely, does not seek its own, is not provoked, thinks no evil; does not rejoice in iniquity, but rejoices in the truth; bears all things, believes all things, hopes all things, endures all things."

~ 1 Corinthians 13:4 - 13:7 (NKJV)

"Work hard so you can present yourself to God and receive His approval. Be a good worker, one who does not need to be ashamed and who correctly explains the Word of Truth!"

~2 Timothy 2:15

"I have a new commandment for you. Love each other the way I have loved you. In doing this, you will prove to the world that you are My disciples."

~ John 13:34,35

When we prove to the world we are His disciples, we are impacting the lives of others. When we lead people to Jesus, fewer people experience Hell for eternity. Speak out and don't be silent. Share your faith with others. Be unashamed!

Stand tall and pronounce your Savior! Give Him the glory and praise He deserves!

Worship Him in everyday life! Don't be ashamed. Love like God as you yield to Him.

"Stand steady and don't be afraid of suffering for The Lord. Bring others to Christ. Leave nothing undone that you ought to do."

~2 Timothy 4:5

We share in enough glory for it to be worth the minimal amount of suffering. What we experience with God is worth the persecutions of the world. Persecution is temporary. Relationship with God lasts forever.

"Go therefore and make disciples of all nations, baptizing them in the name of the Father and of the Son and of the Holy Spirit, teaching them to observe all that I have commanded you. And behold, I am with you always, to the end of the age."

~ Matthew 28:19, 20

Don't let "of nations" throw you off because if you take a look at your genetic background you will find out that you are "of" many nations yourself. We can understand this on terms of it not telling us we have to be a missionary who travels the world necessarily. It means for us to share our faith with others and teach others what Jesus has taught us, wherever we may be. We may share our faith wherever we are, whether it be overseas, down the street, or in our local grocery store. Global missionary work is great! At the same time, we can do missions wherever we are. America has plenty of missions opportunities in it alone. You don't have to go overseas to do God's work!

"Just as the Son of Man did not come to be served but to serve and give His life as a ransom for many."

~ Matthew 20:28

We are to follow Jesus by doing the same. We are meant to serve others rather than expecting others to serve us. At the same time, our one-on-one relationship with God must come first or our service to others won't be as effective as it could be.

Thank you to all who have contributed to this book, Fourth Day Ministries, and the prayer warriors who have helped keep me on my own two feet with eyes set on the prize.

And of course, I THANK JESUS for making all things possible through Him!!!

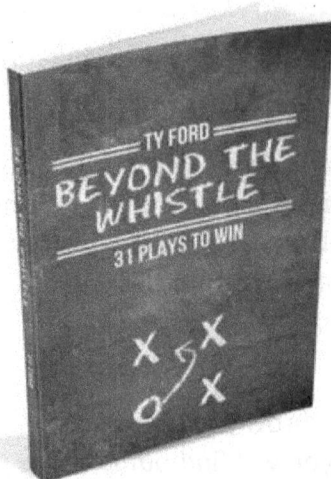

BEYOND THE WHISTLE
31 Plays to Win

Beyond the Whistle is a 31 day devotional designed to jump start your heart in its understanding of God's perfect strength. Your understanding of God's presence in the game of life is crucial because your understanding of your true strength in Christ will determine not only your completion of the game but your success in the choice of plays you make while in the game. This book is the perfect devotional for anyone who is looking to not just play the game of life, but who wants to win. Ty uses the parallels of an athletic playbook and a personal passion to bring scripture to the heart and mind with power and relevance for life on and off the field.

This book may be purchased at www.tyford.org
www.amazon.com

For information on how to book Ty to speak at your church or event, please use the contact tab at www.tyford.org

About the Author

Ty Ford is a husband, father, speaker, former athlete, writer, and author of both THE SOVEREIGNTY OF CHRIST & the 31 Day Devotional, BEYOND THE WHISTLE. He is Pastor and Founder of Fourth Day Ministries. He is an area representative for Fellowship of Christian Athletes (FCA) for East Mississippi. Fourth Day Ministries ministers to the lost, guides people to God's light, and ministers to those in transition from recovery. Fourth Day Ministries has a study bible giving ministry that has given away over 1,000 top of the line study bibles. In Fourth Day Ministries, Ty, his wife Hillary, and some of their friends have ministered the Gospel at multiple different facilities all along the Gulf Coast. They have ministered at Home of Grace in Eight Mile, AL; Mercy House Ministries in Moss Point, MS; and other similar places. Fourth Day Ministries has had a transition house for men where 23 men have come through for extra discipleship, guidance, and assistance in re-entering society. Fourth Day Ministries also has a camp in Meridian, MS where they conduct retreats. The camp used to be used for Girl Scouts, known as Camp Meridale. Now Fourth Day Ministries owns the property. Fourth Day Ministries partners with FCA in hosting camps for sports teams. FCA is a ministry that has access to all schools for the purpose of showing Gods love and bringing the younger generation to Christ. Ty Ford has a passion for God and a purpose that's centered around people. His strongest desires for building God's Kingdom is helping guide people into the will of God while also helping lead them into being sustained in His will. Ty Ford is a man after God's own heart that desires to see people win at life through Christ. Ty Ford is a strong believer that emphasizes to people the importance of reading, studying, meditating, and applying the Word of God to their lives. Ty Ford knows that the key to succeeding in life is dependent upon discipleship and faithfulness.